Augsburg College
George Sverdrup Library
Minneapolis, Minnesota 55404

THE CIVILIZATION OF THE AMERICAN INDIAN SERIES

THE SHADOW OF SEQUOYAH
Social Documents of the Cherokees, 1862–1964

THE SHADOW OF SEQUOYAH

Social Documents
of the Cherokees, 1862-1964

Translated and Edited by
Jack Frederick and Anna Gritts Kilpatrick

UNIVERSITY OF OKLAHOMA PRESS : NORMAN

LIBRARY OF CONGRESS CATALOG CARD NUMBER: 65–24205

Copyright 1965 by the University of Oklahoma Press, Publishing Division of the University. Composed and printed at Norman, Oklahoma, U.S.A., by the University of Oklahoma Press. First edition.

Preface

If there is surprisingly little accurate information in print about the daily life and the intellectual attitudes of the Cherokees, there exists a truly noble corpus of half-truth and nonsense. The Indians that everybody knows about but that almost nobody really knows, it is they, of all the aboriginal people of North America, who have created the most nearly complete self-portrait of an Indian society.

An explanation to this striking paradox is readily to be found in the barrier to the outside world erected by the appallingly difficult Cherokee language that seemingly cannot be mastered by the exercise of will. One speaks Cherokee from the cradle, or one does not speak it. The intense cerebration that it demands extends even those who cannot speak anything else.

The accomplishment of Sequoyah, who about the year 1821 succeeded in providing for his people a practical method of committing their language to writing, has been much and rightly praised, but little has been said about what he failed to do; for with all due respect to the superb feat of this revered ancestor of the junior author of this book, one must confess that the Sequoyah syllabary suffers from grievous shortcomings.

To be specific, the syllabary fails to provide for certain aspects of the Cherokee language that are of critical import: length and pitch of syllables, an intrusive *h*, and the means for distinguishing between voiced and unvoiced vowels. One does not read a document in Cherokee with anything approaching the glibness possible were it written, let us say, in French; for like ancient Egyptian, it must be deciphered. It can readily be seen that considerable reliance must be placed in the authority of context in working with a system of writing that employs, for example, the same two symbols, those for *a* and *ma*, for words as far removed in meaning from each other as *ama* ("water") and *a:ma* ("salt"). Some degree of uncertainty is always present in arriving at the translation of any document in Cherokee.

Manuscripts in Sequoyah ordinarily have no capitalization and no punctuation; the symbols are formed with the widest exercise of personal taste; and spelling, which was never standardized, sometimes touches upon the fantastic. Moreover, there exist several Cherokee dialects, some of which differ from each other almost as radically as Spanish from Portuguese.

Books about the Cherokees have a distressing leaning toward repetition. One reads over and over, for example, that with astonishing rapidity Sequoyah's people became literate after his contribution was made available to them. Seldom in print is one reminded of the sad truth that Sequoyah's syllabary and the whooping crane stand in approximately the same relationship to oblivion. Few indeed are the Cherokees these days who can read and write Cherokee. The spoken language itself faces extinction.

For one hundred years or so after achieving literacy the Cherokee people produced an enormous body of manuscript literature recording nearly every aspect of their culture, and it almost surpasses belief that no one, to our present knowledge, has made a serious attempt to preserve it. Ethnologists and hobbyists, libraries and museums, governmental agencies, and the Cherokee people themselves shared a sublime disinterest. What has apparently survived of this treasure of inestimable value to ethnology, sociology, history, and linguistics consists of but a relatively few, and for the most part poorly preserved, documents, reposing, insofar as we have been able to determine, chiefly in the following depositories: the Bureau of American Ethnology, the Library of the American Philosophical Society, the Library of the University of Oklahoma, the Thomas Gilcrease Museum, and the private collection of these authors.

Thirty years or so ago one might have obtained manuscripts in syllabary by the truckload. Today the average Cherokee cabin is likely to be as devoid of a single scrap of Sequoyan as it is of a copy of Catullus. World War II dealt a deathblow to the way of living of an entire century. Before leaving for opportunity in the city, the young adulthood carried out a tribal housecleaning. Attics and

Preface

trunks were cleared, and into the flames went most of the records of a culture.

But there still remain enough data in the syllabary to present a picture, although admittedly incomplete, of a gifted and sensitive people, whose tragedy has always been that the white man has had no way of truly understanding them. In these pages for once they are permitted to speak for themselves, and if what they say does not jibe with what has been written about them, so much the better. For this privilege they owe an incalculable debt to the kindly shade of Sequoyah.

The phonemic system that we have employed in writing Cherokee with English letters is that devised by Professor Floyd G. Lounsbury, of Yale University, and the senior author at the request of the Bureau of American Ethnology. All English words found in the various manuscripts translated are italicized.

The authors wish to express their profound appreciation to the National Science Foundation for a grant which made possible certain research necessary in the preparation of this book, and to Henry B. Collins, formerly acting director of the Bureau of American Ethnology, and to Professor A. M. Gibson, head, Division of Manuscripts of the University of Oklahoma Library, for making available materials in their respective institutions.

JACK FREDERICK KILPATRICK
ANNA GRITTS KILPATRICK

August 12, 1965
Dallas, Texas

Contents

Preface	vii
Tse:gh(i)sini Disposes of the Effects of a Deceased Comrade-in-Arms (1862)	3
Confederate Tse:gh(i)sini Writes of Home and Honey (1862)	6
Tso:na, Confederate Soldier, Has a Problem at Home (1862)	9
The Thomas Legionnaires Blunder (1863)	10
I:no:li Issues Clothing to Soldiers and to Children of the War Dead (1865)	12
Record of an Epidemic (Smallpox?) at Qualla (1865)	15
I:no:li Disposes of the Affairs of Ulo:nagi:sgi (1867)	16
Mother and Son Dispute in Settling an Estate (1867)	18
List of Purchases by a Union Widow (1867)	20
Apportionment of Land in Wolftown (1869)	21
I:no:li Experiences Boredom in Asheville (1873)	22
Funeral Notice of a Cherokee Methodist Minister (1874)	24
Di:lasge:sgi Reports the Commemoration of the Assassination of Chief Lincoln (1876)	25
Gane:nu:li:sgi Resigns as Solicitor of Goingsnake District (1877)	26
Ezekiel ("Zckc") Proctor Crusades for Good Government (1877)	28
Methodist Revival Notice (1878)	32
Drought-Stricken Citizens Petition Chief Thompson (1879)	33
Tso:wa Hungers for Election News (1881)	34

A Methodist Minister Dies as an Earthquake Is Born (1882) 36
Former Clerk I:no:li Looks Up Death Records (1884) 36
A:l(i)sa Writes to Her Shiftless Husband (ca. 1885) 37
Record of Borrowings from the Treasury of the Eastern
   Band (1885) 39
A Medicine Man and a Minister Write to a Scientist (1888) 40
A Medicine Man's Son Fails to Find Hidden Papers (1888) 42
The Heirs of De:nili O:hla Write to the Judge of Flint
   District (1891) 44
Di:dagw(i) Writes of His Illness (1893) 45
Charm for Assistance in War (1894) 45
The Judge of Goingsnake District Advises Reconciliation
   (1897) 46
Conjuration for Muscular Cramps (1898) 48
Ghe:n(i)di Sv:ghi Necrology (1900–1901) 50
Do:yaní:si Asks Chief Buffington to Identify Him (1901) 52
Address Upon the Keetoowah Society (1901) 53
Memorandum Concerning a Runaway Teen-age Girl
   (1902) 54
Se:dí:hi Fire of the Keetoowah Society Collects Funds for
   Food (1906–1907) 55
"The Panther and the Crane"—A Natchez Cherokee
   Myth (ca. 1908) 57
Vision of a Christian Child (1908) 59
A Cherokee Chronology (ca. 1909) 59
Menu for a Meeting of the Keetoowah Society (1909) 60
Christian Meditations (ca. 1910) 61
Dying Testimony of Cherokee Christians (1910–15) 62
Ani:lage:yv Summarizes His Year in the Vineyard of the
   Lord (1914–15) 65
Fairfield Sunday School Adopts Regulations for the Sick
   and the Dead (1915) 66
Letter from Redbird Smith (1917) 68
An Apprentice Medicine Man Goes to War (1918) 68
Two Love Incantations (ca. 1919) 70

Contents

Record of Money Collected by A:mó:hi Fire of the Keetoowah Society (1919)	70
Notation by a Conjurer Concerning a Female Client (ca. 1920)	71
De:wi AɁhw(i)gado:ga Has a Transportation Problem (1923)	72
List of Repentants at the Quarterly Meeting at Echota Church (ca. 1925)	73
A Gospel Song in Syllables (ca. 1925)	74
Echota Sunday School Makes Plans for the Coming Year (1926)	75
A Backslider Changes His Church Affiliation (1928)	76
Echota Sunday School Decides to Have a Cake Sale (1929)	76
Election of Sergeants-at-Arms (ca. 1930)	77
Hymn Book of U:ne:sdala (ca. 1930)	78
"Going to the Water" Prayer for Longevity (1930)	80
A Temperance Song (ca. 1935)	82
Prescription for Cardiac Disease (1936)	82
Fragment of a Minute Book Recording a Revival at Sycamore Tree Church (1936)	83
Sycamore Tree Church Agrees to Supply Workers for a Convention at Echota Church (1938)	85
A Bundle of Love Letters (1938–39)	86
Diagnoses of a Medicine Man (ca. 1940)	88
Prayer for Divining with Lead (ca. 1940)	89
Comment upon World War II (1940)	90
Letter from the Chief of the Keetoowah Society (1941)	90
Two Children's Remedies (1942)	91
Lu:si Reports on the Illness of U:sgogi:d(a) (1942)	93
Letters from a Patient in Claremore Indian Hospital (1943)	93
Fragment of a Myth (1944)	95
Uwe:da:sadh(i) Writes of Fence Posts and Thieves (1945)	96
A Medicine Man's Dream (1946)	97
Diary Comments upon the Moon and Money (1946)	99
Letter About Fishing-Pole Cane and Health (1947)	100

A Cherokee Recalls to Mind the Alliance of 1730 (1948)   101
Regulations for the Observance of Memorial Day at
    Sycamore Tree Cemetery (1955)   102
The Pastor of Echota Church Writes to One of His
    Deacons (1957)   103
Minutes of Echota Sunday School (1959)   103
Salo:li Broods over the Destiny of the Cherokees (1963)   104
Letters from a Christian Medicine Man (1963)   105
A Baptist Minister's Dream (1963)   107
Gana:hw(i)so:sg(i) Recalls the World War I Parade
    Ground (1964)   107
Bibliography   109
Index   113

REPRODUCTIONS OF CHEROKEE DOCUMENTS

Gane:nu:li:sgi Resigns as Solicitor of Goingsnake District   27
Ezekiel Proctor Crusades for Good Government   30–31
Drought-Stricken Citizens Petition Chief Thompson   33
Do:yaní:si Asks Chief Buffington to Identify Him   51

THE SHADOW OF SEQUOYAH
Social Documents of the Cherokees, 1862–1964

Tse:gh(i)sini Disposes of the Effects of a Deceased Comrade-in-Arms (1862)

The Civil War did not have the same significance to the Western Cherokees as it did to their tribesmen who had refused to be bound by the fraudulent Treaty of New Echota in 1835 and since the Removal of 1838–39 had been precariously existing near their old homes, first as hunted outlaws in the Smoky Mountains and later as squatters on the lands of their protector and unofficial white chief, Will Thomas.[1] The Cherokee Nation in the West came apart along the line of a pre-existing fracture—the Watie-Boudinot faction that had advocated collaboration with the whites and voluntary removal, and the faction headed by Principal Chief John Ross that had resisted ejection from Georgia, Alabama, Tennessee, and North Carolina to the very end. The North Carolina remnant, solidified by their ghastly past sufferings, supported the Confederacy because Thomas was a Confederate. Almost every able-bodied man among them enlisted in his Thomas Legion, and, as their colonel, he unashamedly protected them as much as he could. Their losses were rather light, and their principal locus at Qualla, one of the loveliest spots upon the face of the globe, was untouched by war. In the West, Union and Confederate Cherokees fought with demonic fury and with the help of their respective allies, white and Indian, did their utmost to depopulate and raze the Cherokee Nation.

By the merest chance a small batch of letters from Thomas

---

[1] The story of this noble white man's relationship to the Cherokees will perhaps never be better told than in Mattie Russell, "William Holland Thomas, White Chief of the Cherokees," doctoral dissertation, Duke University, 1951.

Legionnaires, written in the florid Sequoyan and the highly aberrant dialects peculiar to North Carolina, escaped the tooth of Time and came to rest in the archives of the Bureau of American Ethnology in the Smithsonian Institution, Washington, D. C.[2]

In sharp contrast to the Western Cherokees, many of whom were wealthy slaveholders, the Eastern Cherokees were greatly depressed economically, and there exist documents[3] that record contentions among them, as ridiculous as they are pathetic, over minute sums of money. A penny-counting honesty in financial matters has always been one of the most engaging traits in fullblood Cherokees, to whom a purported lack of it in white men has ever afforded a favorite grievance. One notes here how careful Tse:gh(i)sini is to provide witnesses for such monetary transactions as might incur uncharitable interpretations.

The sum accruing from the auction of the personal effects of the deceased soldier was, of course, in Confederate money, which at this date had a purchasing power of about one-half that of its United States counterpart. Even so, one wonders why these articles went for as much as twenty-eight dollars. Perhaps the buyers, being comrades of the dead soldier and knowing that the proceeds of the sale were destined for the family of the deceased, bid a trifle recklessly.

July 8, 1862

During this year we worked![4]

At 11 o'clock we put up for sale Da:sgigidi:hi's personal effects. These we put up for sale here in Strawberry Plains, Tennessee.

---

[2] An account of how the Bureau of American Ethnology acquired these manuscripts is found in James Mooney, "Sacred Formulas of the Cherokees," *7th Annual Report*, Bureau of American Ethnology (1900), 314–16.

[3] Some of these are translated in Anna Gritts and Jack Frederick Kilpatrick, "Chronicles of Wolftown: Social Documents of the North Carolina Cherokees," scheduled for publication by the Bureau of American Ethnology, and hereinafter cited as "Chronicles of Wolftown."

[4] Apparently the writer is defending his tardiness in writing home.

Now!⁵ This is the amount that we sold—$28.00's worth.

I have sent $30.00 to help out. It does not appear to include my $2.00, but this is what I just thought: there was a white hat over there⁶ that I was to get, I think, and I will pay for it soon, if you don't sell it. If you have not sold it, I:no:li, I give you permission to deduct my $2.00. Tsumi, U:gama, and Sdhu:gado:ga⁷ are witnesses that I paid on it.

No! Tell us the right thing to do.⁸ We did the right thing, I suppose. A different man helped me, Tse:gh(i)sini.⁹ The reason was, Di:ghuyi:sgi¹⁰ was sick.

Now! That which was owed him¹¹ you do not find as an asset here. His debtors have paid a small amount, it appears. There were witnesses that he was paid, and that is why I have given up.¹² Then that is not all that I see in this matter. It makes me hurry too fast. It is plain that I must write you another letter soon. I will tell you all about it. I finished the one I started, but someone else owes him. I will start again.¹³

Now! This white man who lives away off at the edge of the place we call Rabbit¹⁴ is keeping my new hammers for me. I have given him permission to use them at his home.

---

⁵ While *gha?* has a variety of meanings, it is most commonly used in writing to preface a new thought. There are other words in Cherokee for "now" used in an adverbial sense.

⁶ At Qualla.

⁷ Fellow soldiers. As will be seen in another document, two of the three, Tsumi and Sdhu:gado:ga, later died for the Confederacy.

⁸ I:no:li, the recipient of the letter, was a revered figure as well as a relative, being a medicine man, a Methodist minister, and an official of Wolftown, one of the townships at Qualla (see Mooney, "Sacred Formulas of the Cherokees," *7th Annual Report*, Bureau of American Ethnology [1900], 314-15).

⁹ The reference must be to helping arrange the auction.

¹⁰ This individual was probably a noncommissioned officer who normally would have taken charge of the sale.

¹¹ The deceased soldier.

¹² The writer's meaning here appears to be: "Since his financial transactions were witnessed, I did not attempt to settle all of his affairs."

¹³ This is obscure, but perhaps "this letter and a second one to follow" is what the writer has in mind.

¹⁴ We cannot identify this place. It was probably near Qualla, of course.

Now! This is all of what you asked me about that I want to make known, I:no:li. Now I have stopped writing.[15]

Do:tsulé:ʔhnv says that small effects I can return.

Today I am not well, but I am alive. Tso:wa is well now; Wi:ligi is well now. Tsa:n(i)lo:si is quite sick, but La:hw(i)sini and I are still alive now.

Now! This April 3rd Su:le died. He was lost at Standingwater.[16] There have been five burials since we came here.

Now! We are greeting you from where we are out here, I:no:li and your aunt, E:ni. You have been waiting on me for a long time. Finally, now, this is it.

Now! I, Tse:gh(i)sini, scribbled[17] this. It appears that I am well now. My friends are very sick.[18]

CONFEDERATE TSE:GH(I)SINI WRITES OF
HOME AND HONEY (1862)

This letter from the same young North Carolina Cherokee Confederate who wrote the preceding missive proves that which stands in little need of proof—that the date of the war and the color of the uniform are of but small consequence: a soldier's soul is filled with yearning for faces from home, girls, and a change from the repulsive results of camp cooking.

The writer of the letter and its recipient were near-relatives —a circumstance favorable to the recording of a concern with minutiae such as: the purchase (with which we are already familiar) of a hat on credit, sickness on the home front, romantic gossip, camp visits, war news (true and false), food, and the well-being of relatives.

Any of the foregoing might be found in any letter in any language from any soldier in any army engaged in any war.

It is a pleasure to record that, insofar as the admittedly in-

---

[15] Cherokee letter writing abounds in false stops such as this.

[16] While we cannot identify this place with certainty, it was between Qualla and Knoxville.

[17] The calligraphy is exceptionally neat.

[18] MS in Inoli, "The Inoli Letters," MS No. 2236, Folder 1. Bureau of American Ethnology. Hereinafter cited as "The Inoli Letters."

complete records in "The Inoli Letters" show, the engaging Tse:gh(i)sini apparently survived both homesickness and battle, returned home, and, no doubt to his joy, dropped out of history.

July 20, 1862

I just wrote this out here at Strawberry Plains, Tennessee, to Wolftown,[1] located on Qualla Cherokee Reservation in Jackson County,[2] North Carolina.

I:no:li, allow me to write you at this time, Sunday evening. I am getting along well.

Now! A few days ago I sent you a letter giving you permission to get the hat. I forget to tell you to let me know quickly if you were able to do what I asked you to do. If I get the letter, and those from over there[3] that are here are still here, I will send the money by them. You can see it again![4] This I think I want to know—what you have done about what I asked you to do.

Now! I also want to know how those quite a few sick at home are getting along. We believe that someone has gone to search for someone.[5] You tell me that, too.

Now! For us to visit you is a hopeless situation, even though we do want to visit you. But then he[6] mentions our moving nearer to the mountains[7] that he keeps talking about. It appears that we are still going to come.

He finally said this morning, "Not long from now, when I leave, it will be nearer for them to see all of you friends, and for me to see them." This he said. And then he spoke again, "If the Yankees are near here, then that is just the way it is: we can't move." This Will Thomas said.

[1] Wolftown (Wahhyó:hi) is the easternmost township on the Qualla Reservation. Its name undoubtedly derives from the fact that it originally was a settlement of members of the Wolf Clan.
[2] In 1862 county lines crossed the Qualla holdings.
[3] From Qualla, across the Smoky Mountains.
[4] An idiom for "you will be paid."
[5] An idiom for "to look for a wife."
[6] Col. Will Thomas.
[7] The Smoky Mountains to the east.

If our leaving is put off for some time, then you yourselves will have to come, and we will see each other. Those who live at Cheowa[8] sometimes come; for it is nearer than where you all live. Don't let anything keep you from coming, if you want all of us friends to see each other.

Now! Since the war started, in fighting everywhere they have decreased us. Our ranks were decreased by 10,000; we decreased the Yankees by 30,000. They counted all of them, and they told us that that was all that were lost. Not very many were decreased from the ranks of our side.[9] This is what the Northern leader[10] stated. One would think that he would be more than ready to give up!

Now! This is what I think: since I cannot come myself, you can do this for me. At the present we are talking to each other by means of a letter. It has been long ago now since we personally talked to each other. Now from where I am out here, I am asking you for honey. If you give it to me, I have asked those who are from over there visiting La:hw(i)sini to bring me a canteen[11] of it, or if they have jars, several jarsful of it. I am not asking it free. I will pay you the full price. Write me how much it is, and I will pay you.

Now! Now I have just stopped writing. I hope that you are well *v:ghini:li*[12] I:no:li, and all of your family. I am well—and

---

[8] Although politically members of the Eastern Band, the Cheowa Cherokees on Snowbird Creek in Graham County, North Carolina, have maintained their isolation since the Removal days. Apparently they were originally closer related to some of the Cherokees who went west than to their neighbors at Qualla. Their peculiar dialect probably has some affinity to Itsodí:yi, a speech of western Adair County, Oklahoma.

[9] Statistical scuttlebutt is an ubiquitous element in military camplife in any war.

[10] The reference here may be to President Lincoln, but it is more likely that it is to some Union general.

[11] One may obtain a concept of the problems of the translators from an examination of the literal meaning of this word: "the-handled-container-that-shines soldiers-they to-carry-them-(solid)-they."

[12] This can mean older brother, father's brother's son older than the user of the term, mother's sister's son older than the user of the term, father's sister's

Grandmother E:ni is well, I suppose. I became wide awake when I just read your letter about how you all are getting along. I keep seeing you, Grandmother, the way you spoke! I believe that you would get wide awake, I:no:li, if you read a letter from your mother and aunt!

Now! I greet you this evening from far away.

Now! I, Tse:gh(i)sini, just scribbled this. I am well. You also, I suppose. How are all the women at home getting along? Very well?

Now! I greet you this evening.[13]

TSO:NA, CONFEDERATE SOLDIER, HAS A PROBLEM AT HOME (1862)

The Cherokees themselves recognize "that legalistic turn of mind, with its tenacity for proprietary and monetary rights"[1] that gives them a folk-reputation for contentiousness—especially among themselves, with whom, of course, they chiefly deal. In some respects they are certainly to be reckoned among the most generous and least grasping people upon the globe, but the spirit of compromise flies out the window at the mere breathing of that most hackneyed word in the Cherokee language—*duyu:gh(o)dv* ("right"): for Principle has reared its head.[2]

"You know that what has happened is not right," fulminates the soldier in the following letter, but we do not know whether he is raising the question of *duyu:gh(o)dv* before I:no:li in the latter's capacity as Wolftown official, minister of the gospel, relative, or friend. We do know that the salt was not granu-

---

son older than the user of the term, and father's mother's brother's son older than the user of the term (see William Harlen Gilbert, Jr., *The Eastern Cherokees*, Bureau of American Ethnology *Bulletin 133*, Anthropological Paper No. 23 [1943], 216–89).

[13] MS in "The Inoli Letters."

[1] Kilpatrick and Kilpatrick, "Chronicles of Wolftown."

[2] There is much truth in the seriocomic statement: ". . . the division of any estate is almost certain to engender a feud. Legacies of gourd dippers and three-legged chairs are capable of raising mighty issues involving *duyu:gh(o)dv*."—Jack Frederick Kilpatrick, *The Friends of Thunder*, 99.

lated but in the form of bars, for some Cherokee verb forms specify in their subjects qualities such as length, liquidity, limpness, and the like.

And we feel certain that the woman who misappropriated the salt—morally undergirded, no doubt, by her own unshakable private concept of *duyu:gh(o)dv*—was a close relative.

July 22, 1862

Now! Now I, Tso:na, will write.

This salt of mine at Qualla, they took. You know that what has happened is not right. I heard that Tsu:di got it. This is not what should have happened.

You get for my sister Ne:n(i)si her part of it. I lived at Ne:n(i)si Gana:gilv's. She came to see me.[3] I consider her to be the only one that is kind. I grew up there. This Tsu:di does not believe anything I say.

Tsu:di, don't be feeling good while you are nibbling my salt! (Ne:n(i)si Gana:gilv went by there.)[4]

Remain there, and I will come. It will make me feel good when we see each other. All of you stay there at Ne:n(i)si Gana:gilv's.

Now! I:no:li, I have just told you that you must talk to them convincingly. It is Ne:n(i)si that is to get the salt.

Now! That is all that it became necessary for me to write. Now I have just stopped writing.

I, Tso:na

This is I:no:li's letter.[5]

The Thomas Legionnaires Blunder (1863)

The Cherokee companies in the Thomas Legion were especially utilized in hunting down deserters, enemy scouts, bushwhackers, and bands of Union sympathizers who had holed up in the mountains. Anyone who has an acquaintance with

---

[3] At Strawberry Plains, most probably.
[4] And found Tsu:di in possession of the salt?
[5] MS in "The Inoli Letters."

Social Documents of the Cherokees, 1862–1964

the Smoky Mountains can readily appreciate the difficulty of the work, but then anyone who knows Cherokees is familiar with their consummate woodsmanship. Union brass inveighed haughtily against Confederate military morals in employing Indians for such police work.

The letter here gives a clear picture of the nature of the duty to which Qualla troops were assigned. It is full of soldier slang. To Cherokees, the funniest jokes are on themselves, and the writer bubbles with amusement over a skirmish that involved friends versus friends. In what spirit the individual who was shot received the jest we can but surmise, but it is safe to assume that his merriment was restrained.

August 3, 1863

Now! We are over here in North Carolina now. We just came into town.[1] We started from Tennessee a week ago. You are a fibber about how long we are staying.[2] I don't know how long we are to remain. All we know is when we get ready to leave.

We have brought in 29 Yankee pretenders.[3] Two are resting on the mountain where they were staying. We made them stop their wrong-doing on Monday. On Tuesday another one rested; Thursday another one rested.

On last Tuesday quite a few guns were sounding. They[4] were told that there were quite a few Yankees nearby and that they would fight very soon. Those were the only ones we looked for.

We saw them for sure, and then we began soldiering around.[5] There was a house 200 feet away. While others in the underbrush waited in ambush, some of us were ordered to attack the white house. Then when they found out that we were Indians,

---

[1] There is no clue in the letter to the name of this town.

[2] Perhaps I:no:li had made a prediction.

[3] The exact meaning of this slang term of a century ago is seemingly irrecoverable, but it may refer to Unionists posing as Confederates.

[4] The Thomas Legionnaires.

[5] Cherokee verbs have a special form for expressing an action done habitually in a somewhat offhand manner.

they came out of the house and ran and hid. One could see their hats bobbing.

Then Ge:dini[6] ordered them to halt. Twice he ordered them to halt. He became quite angry. Then they halted.

Guns were hidden in the house. Those that were outside we took away from them.

Later on, we talked to them. We gave them back what we had lifted from them. They were our allies! We were not told that they were on our side. If we had been told, or if they had said, "Here are your allies!" we wouldn't have had that scrap.

We wounded one, but he didn't die. We didn't recognize each other was the reason this happened. We decided it was a joke; but if we had killed one another, then that would have been very bad, they said. Ha! We made a joke!

Now! What I told you, I:no:li, what you saw in this letter, don't tell your friends.[7]

We are all getting along well. Sickness can catch you. When it catches you, are not well, but one can send this root.[8]

Now! That is all that I, Do:tsulé:ʔhnv, just wrote.

I am getting along well. I send my greetings from away off.[9]

I:NO:LI ISSUES CLOTHING TO SOLDIERS AND TO CHILDREN OF THE WAR DEAD (1865)

Being abysmally poor to begin with, the Eastern Cherokees experienced much home-front privation while their menfolk were fighting for the Confederacy. From various manuscript

---

[6] Probably a noncommissioned officer.

[7] The writer was somewhat abashed and no doubt feared ridicule from friends and relatives.

[8] Other references in the collection from which this letter came make one suspect that the writer was studying to be a medicine man. In later life I:no:li, the recipient of the letter and the medicinal root that accompanied it, was a shaman (see Mooney, "Sacred Formulas of the Cherokees," 7th *Annual Report*, Bureau of American Ethnology [1900], 315), but in 1863 he, too, was probably still a student. The wording of this passage suggests a professional caution stemming from the possibility of its coming before the eye of the uninitiated.

[9] MS in "The Inoli Letters."

sources[1] we learn that at times the women, children, and elders at Qualla barely skirted starvation, and only their remarkable knowledge of edible barks, berries, roots, and foliage saved them. They were always in need of clothing.

But as usual, they could count upon the friendship of Will Thomas. With Confederate finances being what they were, Colonel Thomas found it necessary to buy with personal funds food and clothing for his Indian troops and their destitute families.

The document below would appear to be the record of an issuance of clothing purchased by Thomas for some of the men in Company C of the Thomas Legion and for the children of those who died while serving in this unit. The number of the dead in this one company, incidentally, does not quite bear out Mooney's statement relative to the paucity of casualties among soldiers from Qualla.[2]

I, I:no:li,[3] on February 13, 1865 issued clothes to my soldiers. They are to pay for them themselves.[4]

Ne:di received	$16.00
Ga:gama received	10.00
U:l(i)sdu:hi received	114.00
A:matsv:na received	16.00
Gwe:ni received	9.00
Tse:gwadi:hi received	6.00
Di:gini received	10.00
AʔhwƗ(i)gado:ga received	6.50
Tsu:hla received	8.00
Dida:lidó:gi received	6.00
Se:luwo:ya received	10.00
Ts(i)sgili received	10.00
Tsa:n(i)la:tsi received	12.00

[1] Russell, "William Holland Thomas," 398; "The Inoli Letters," *passim.*
[2] Mooney, *Myths of the Cherokee,* 170.
[3] I:no:li himself joined the Thomas Legion in 1863 and became a sergeant.
[4] Although the clothing must have been issued with the understanding that Thomas was to be reimbursed when the soldiers drew long overdue pay, one doubts that the Confederacy ever settled its account.

Galu:sadi:hi received	6.00
Gahu:ni received	12.00
Da:dhlvda received	6.00
Wa:sida?ni received	12.00
U:dhlvna:da received	6.00
Wo:yigvgi:sgi received	6.00
Tsutso:ladha received	7.50

I, I:no:li, wrote this on February 14, 1865. I counted the orphaned children of those soldiers killed. The number of clothes they received free:

Sdugi:gado:ga*	Ne:tsili†	6‡	18§
Ni:gi	Ne:ni	5	18||
Anidó:na?	Gvwahyu:da	1	3
U:dan(i)dhu:da	Tsi:guwi	1	3
Tsuda:sodi	Wali:sa	5	15
Gv:na	Ani:tsa	3	9
Tsa:li	Sina:sdhv	7	21
Gv:hnidv	Tsiyv:lv:da	7	21
Di:ye:lidó:hi	Hv:yvli	7	21

* The deceased soldiers are listed in this column.

† The names in this column appear to be chiefly those of the wives of the deceased soldiers, thus those of a few males *in loco parentis* to the children of deceased soldiers (maternal uncles, grandfathers).

‡ The number of surviving children.

§ The number of articles of clothing.

\|\| Apparently an error for 15. One can see that the procedure was to allot each child three articles of clothing.

Now! This is the number of those who died of disease:

Dvni:gisi	Ne:di	1	3
Ha:li	Ni:gudayi	3	9
Ga:yani	[?]#	1	3
Uli:da:sdi	Ghe:ladi	3	9
Si?duwe:gi	Gado:tsv:na	2	6
Dasgi:gidi:hi	Tsulo:gila	1	3
Ama:y(i)gado:ga	Ghv:he	3	9

Do:sagaya:sdi	Agwade:gi	1	3
Tsumi	A:nuwe:gi	3	9
Sgali:lo:sgi	Sa:dayi	6	18
Godagwa:sgi	E:ni	5	15
Tsa:ts(a)	Agiló:hi	2	6
Oga?hnawa	A:li Wadi:sgi	4	12
Ule:na:hi	Ghv:he	3	9
I:nadv	Hv:gi	4	12
Digv:gi:sgi	A:yele	5	15
Wahhyaní:da	Ul(i)sga:sdi	3	9
Da:hw(i)sini	Li:di	1	3
Diwo:sgi	Li:la	1	3**

\# A name must have been inadvertently omitted here.
** MS in "The Inoli Letters."

RECORD OF AN EPIDEMIC (SMALLPOX?) AT QUALLA (1865) Smallpox, brought by slave traders to Charleston and from there conveyed to the Cherokee country in trade goods, destroyed nearly half of the Cherokee people in 1738.[1] Other epidemics, occuring as late as the present century, also resulted in extensive loss of life among the Western Cherokees.

Incidentally, Adair's account[2] of the early Cherokee attempts to cure smallpox, much quoted, is exceedingly unreliable. Having small insight into Cherokee medical practice, it is all too obvious that Adair grievously misinterpreted what little firsthand information that he possessed and eked out his narration with traders' gossip. His account should be accepted with caution.

Mooney states that about thirty of the North Carolina Cherokee soldiers deserted and served in the Union Army. One of those who did so, upon returning home after demobilization, brought the smallpox with him, and over one hundred of his tribesmen succumbed to it.

The same authority states that this epidemic was in the spring of 1866, but it may have actually begun in the previous fall inasmuch as this list of deaths, jotted by I:no:li upon the

[1] Williams, *Adair's History of the American Indians*, 244-46.
[2] *Ibid.*

verso of a conjuration, shows an exceedingly large number of deaths occurring during a single month in a community as small as Wolftown.³

It became necessary for me to write this—the number of Wolftown residents who died in October of this year, 1865:
Da:tsvda. . . . He served as a soldier with I:no:li⁴
Ule:yoe (from something)⁵ . . . He served as a soldier with I:no:li
Ts(i)sgo:yi
Hv:wo:di
Gwe:dh(i)si⁶ (from something)
A:ligi
La:hw(i)sini.⁷ . . . He was a soldier
Tsadha:g(a)nihyv:ga. . . . He served as a soldier with I:no:li
De:gi
Tsulo:gila
Nigula:ni
Hv:wo:ni:sgi
Ne:n(i)si
Tso:na
Go:liwa:ni⁸

I:NO:LI DISPOSES OF THE AFFAIRS OF
ULO:NASGI:SGI (1867)

The Cherokees have a folk belief that they are especially vul-

---

³ Mooney, *Myths of the Cherokee*, 171-72.

⁴ In Company C, 69th North Carolina Volunteer Infantry (The Thomas Legion).

⁵ Dead from some unknown cause?

⁶ Other documents in our possession indicate that this was I:no:li's mother.

⁷ This individual served in some company other than that in which I:no:li served. He was in Tse:gh(i)sini's company (see "Tse:gh(i)sini Disposes of the Effects of a Deceased Comrade-in-Arms [1862]").

⁸ MS in "Inali Formulae," "Inali" is yet another attempt by cataloguers to arrive at a spelling with English phonemic values of the name that in the Lounsbury-Kilpatrick System we render "I:no:li."

nerable to arthritis, gall stones,[1] and urinary disorders; and indeed, in the large body of manuscript medical writings in the Bureau of American Ethnology, the Library of the American Philosophical Society, and the library of the authors, treatments for these conditions are strongly represented. The seemingly high incidence of urinary ailments among the North Carolina Cherokees of the period of the following letter has been ascribed, perhaps unscientifically, to the extensive use by these Indians of wood-ash lye as a condiment in cooking.

Where the recipient of this letter lived is not known, although one suspects that it was Cheowa; nor is it ever explained why the deceased Ulo:nasgi:sgi had been in South Carolina, which in 1867 had no settlement of Cherokees, so far as we know. Even how I:no:li, the writer of the letter, reobtained possession of it is a minor mystery; it was found among his papers.

To our way of thinking, the chief interest in the document is the solicitude of the survivors in liquidating the debts of the deceased. Auctions of effects of the dead in order to pay off debts were a phase of Cherokee life, both in North Carolina and Oklahoma, up until a generation or so ago. Detailed records exists of such sales at Qualla at the approximate period of this letter.[2]

April 12, 1867

It became necessary for me to write for those who live here[3] in Jackson County, North Carolina, sister[4] Ahu:yv.

Now! I suppose that you heard that Ulo:nasgi:sgi was sick when he came here to Qualla from South Carolina. Ama:-yigado:ga Gana:gilv said that he fell. He was urinating blood,

---

[1] The medical officer in charge of a government hospital in Oklahoma once informed us that his experience would tend to indicate that Cherokees are more than twice as susceptible to gallstones than is the general public.

[2] Kilpatrick and Kilpatrick, "Chronicles of Wolftown."

[3] I:no:li must have meant that in his capacity as clerk of Wolftown he recorded the death of Ulo:nasgi:sgi.

[4] The term used here could also mean father's brother's daughter or mother's sister's daughter. In any event, she was undoubtedly a relative of the deceased, as well as of I:no:li.

he said. I actually saw the pants that he wore. They were very bloody.

He died on April 8th. Just at dark his life stopped, and we fixed him up with a good coffin.

Now! That is all that I have to say.

Now! The few personal effects that he had will be sold. He owed $7.11.[5]

So that you could hear about it quickly, I made this letter this way. You must quickly send me your thinking about what is in this letter in a letter for me, I:no:li, to read.

[*on verso*]

Now! Now I just wrote[6] that Ghan(i)si:ni died on Sunday, December 1st.[7]

Mother and Son Dispute in Settling an Estate (1867)

Here we observe what must have been a fairly typical case of the intramural strife that frequently rose to trouble the official nostrils of Wolftown. It was formerly the custom for the township itself to inventory and conduct auction sales of the possessions of those deceased, and there is ample evidence that tempers rose before this effect or that was allowed to go under the hammer.

We sense from the clerk's terminology that, as far as he was personally concerned, he leaned toward the case of the surviving spouse; for, according to Cherokee custom, the mother had a superior right deriving from her having been the member of the family who nursed the deceased during his terminal illness. Neither the fact that she was the wife of the deceased nor the matricentered aspect of the Cherokee household (much overplayed in the printed literature) carried much weight. The son (or he may have been a stepson), although

---

[5] If it were not for the fact that the man was ill, the size of his indebtedness, by North Carolina Cherokee standards of 1867, might give rise to suspicions of riotous living.

[6] I.e., "I am writing." Cherokee has a recent past tense, very difficult to translate without the overuse of "just."

[7] MS in "The Inoli Letters."

living at home as stated, being eldest, had even less inherent right to property than did a younger child who also may have been living at home; for the Cherokees generally adhere to the principle of ultimogeniture.[1]

We are left to wonder about what eventually happened to the field of corn, but an inspection of the inventory of the possessions of the late E:sigi is some compensation for our uncertainty. E:sigi indeed was poor, we must conclude, but his estate probably differed little from that which many a white North Carolinian mountaineer might have left to raise among his heirs the white man's version of *duyu:gh(o)dv.*

Now! It became necessary to write this on August 1, 1867.

Le:gini, who is a good citizen, has just come to me and said, "E:sigi is dead, and he left some effects, and also some corn still growing in the field. The first-born boy thinks this is his. I take care of him," she said.

E:sigi Ge:layi:ni's wife says that the corn still growing in the field is hers also, and that she is ready to take care of affairs right. She counted everything that E:sigi left.

I counted all the clothes and pots.

1. A black coat.
2. Some short blue cloth.
3. Some belted soldier's clothing.[2]
4. Some quilts.
5. Some quilts.
6. A Dutch oven.
7. A Dutch oven.
8. A brass lock.
9. A horse-drawn plow.
10. An ax.
11. A hoe. It belonged to Gwe:gi. He [E:sigi] still owed for it. She [Le:gini] said that she had been asked for payment.

[1] See Gilbert, *The Eastern Cherokees*, 307.
[2] Probably Confederate.

12. A knife.
13. Two pounds of cotton. She says that she still owes the nearby store in Jackson [County] for it.

She owes all of these a little:[3]

She owes in Jackson [County]	$2.50
She owes Sa:dayi	.20
She owes Sigwi:ya A:matsv:na	.10
She owes the white man's store nearby	.05

I know that these owe her a little:[4]

Gho:gv owes	$1.40
Tsimi owes	1.25[5]

LIST OF PURCHASES BY A UNION WIDOW (1867)

In comparison with the usual monetary transaction at Qualla, this inventory of purchases by a Western Cherokee of the corresponding period reads like a venture into high finance. The economy of Qualla was based upon trading-post bartering; there were those in the Cherokee Nation who attended Ivy League schools and whose footmen wore livery.[1]

From documents in our possession we learn that the purchaser of the items below was the widow of a Cherokee Union soldier of Co. D, 2nd Regiment of the Indian Home Guards who fell at the Battle of Cabin Creek (July 1–3, 1863). She lived somewhere in that part of Goingsnake District that is now northern Adair County.

$50.00 — paid for a field[2]
50.00 — paid for a horse
30.00 — paid for steers
 8.00 — paid for a cow
 8.00 — paid for pigs

[3] Debts of her late husband.
[4] Debtors of her late husband.
[5] MS in "The Inoli Letters."
[1] See Carolyn Thomas Foreman, *Park Hill, passim.*
[2] While in the Cherokee Nation one could not buy land itself, a crop growing upon it could be purchased.

Social Documents of the Cherokees, 1862–1964

1.50 — paid for a pig
5.00 — paid for all[3]
.25 — paid for something I got at the store

This which is written down, and for which they[4] extended me credit, I paid for in full today.

A:li Wa:dh(i)

I just wrote this October 8, 1867[5]

Apportionment of Land in Wolftown (1869)

In 1869 the title to the approximately fifty thousand acres of land upon which the Cherokees were living at Qualla became clouded. Creditors of the benefactor of the Indians, Will Thomas, had through sheriff's deeds acquired all of the Thomas Qualla holdings. It appeared that the lands that had largely been purchased with their own money, but which had been held in Thomas' name because of the state laws that prohibited the original inhabitants of North Carolina from owning any of their own soil, were lost to the Cherokees. But the might of the United States government was waiting in the wings, prepared to step in and give the Indians a legal home at last.[1]

During the murky negotiations of 1869–70 that involved state and federal governments, the Thomas estate and the creditors thereof, the civic machinery of Wolftown purred on serenely. We find in this document in the handwriting of Clerk I:no:li that probably with more expedition, and certainly with less expense than could have been done by either state or federal government, it ironed out the question concerning which householder was entitled to live where.

One notes that some of the names on this roll are feminine—widows, no doubt. The figure opposite each name would appear to represent tracts of land.

---

[3] A number of miscellaneous items?
[4] We have no information concerning who "they" were. Perhaps A:li bought an estate.
[5] MS in collection of authors.
[1] Mooney, *Myths of the Cherokee*, 173.

THE SHADOW OF SEQUOYAH

Here at Qualla we just met and made a decision on June 21, 1869.

Now! Chief Ts(i)sgili asked me to write this.

Now on June 21st all of them that live here at Qualla were asked individually what each desired to own all the time.[2] One can read how it was done here in Wolftown. They all think it is equitable.

Ts(i)sgili	3
U:l(i)se?go:gí:dv	2
Di:ghuyi:sgi	1
U:l(i)sdu:[hi]	2
U:wawo:sidi	1
Di:gahl(u)ghwade:gi	2
Ge:si	2
Tsa:n(i)la:tsi	2
Tsa:li	2
Dvdi:sdv	2
Tsi:ni	1
A:nuwe:gi	2
O:yasdv	1
Wa:sida?ni	2
Tsutso:ladha	2
Utse:nadha	2
A?hw(i)daya:i	1
Wi:l(i)sini	2
Salo:lani	1
I:no:li	1
Gwe:di	1[3]

I:NO:LI EXPERIENCES BOREDOM IN ASHEVILLE (1873)

To an Indian from Qualla, Asheville in 1873 must have been as alien and unsympathetic as Uranus. It is evident that the

---

[2] This apportionment was, we assume, a step toward the establishment of a tribal government on December 1, 1870.
[3] MS in "The Inoli Letters."

writer of this note to his family back home was not enjoying his metropolitan visit. He probably was a witness in an action brought by a faction of the Eastern Band against Will Thomas for the purpose of forcing Thomas to account for tribal moneys that he had handled between the years 1836 and 1861.[1] It is evident that the writer, putting first things first, was primarily concerned with getting his patch of wheat planted. Wheat was wheat; but the mountains of legal papers in the white man's court, whatever potentiality for riches that they might have held, were at the moment indigestible.

1873

Now! It just became necessary for me to write.

I stay here in Asheville uselessly. I have remained here a long time. There is nothing to be done. Still they say that we will leave Sunday, and it appears to be true that we will return then.

I am not well yet but I am walking, not quite as well as all of you.

Tso:saya,[2] you plant that wheat in the ground, I say. That is all that I tell you.

Now! I suppose that those papers[3] are all wrapped up in a black handkerchief in the bedroom. When someone comes for them, it will be good if he takes them to Wi:l(i)sini's house.

Now! That is all that I, I:no:li, just wrote for you, Gado:yoe, Sa:li, and Tso:saya to hear.

We all are leaving Sunday, it appears.

[on verso]

Gado:yoe's[4] letter.[5]

---

[1] Russell, "William Holland Thomas," 420.

[2] I:no:li's son (see "A:l(i)sa Writes to Her Shiftless Husband [ca. 1885].")

[3] Apparently these papers have no relationship to the court action at Asheville.

[4] This feminine member of the writer's family was probably a daughter, and the only member who could read Cherokee.

[5] MS in "The Inoli Letters."

FUNERAL NOTICE OF A CHEROKEE METHODIST MINISTER (1874)

Although reliable statistics are not available, it is incontestable that among Cherokee Christians the Baptist denomination predominates, with the Methodist in second place. In Oklahoma there are some forty-four churches of the one sect,[1] fourteen of the other; at Qualla the proportion is eleven to two.[2]

We do not have denominational statistics for Qualla for the year 1874, but we suspect that Methodism was relatively stronger then than it is at present. At that time Echota Methodist Mission on Soco Creek in Wolftown was a stronghold of Christianity, and documents still in existence serve to attest to its force in the lives of the North Carolina Cherokees. One of these documents, translated here, is the funeral notice of a native minister associated with the mission.

Cherokee funeral notices are customarily handprinted upon any suitable scrap of paper or cardboard available, sometimes decorated with fanciful elaborations of the Sequoyah syllable-symbols, and with vignettes, in the creation of which one senses hours of grief-beguiling make-work. In Oklahoma, and probably in North Carolina also, when someone died during the night, it was traditional to tack a notice to the church door at sunrise and to ring the church bell so that the community might inform itself of the name of the deceased and the particulars of the forthcoming funeral. If the death occurred during the day, the notice was posted and the bell tolled at sundown. Although moribund, this practice is not yet extinct in Oklahoma Cherokeeia.

Oklahoma funeral notices frequently call for volunteer gravediggers;[3] and in addition to routine reporting of the names and ages of the deceased, they convey appraisals of work for the Kingdom, last words, and states of grace before departure.

The funeral notice here is an uncommonly ornate one. Its wording, in handprinting of various sizes, is spaced out in the

---

[1] Personal communication by Rev. Leslie Smith, Tahlequah, Oklahoma.
[2] John Gulick, *Cherokees at the Crossroads*, 36.
[3] Jack Frederick Kilpatrick, "Echota Funeral Notices," MS.

style of a handbill. Some of its larger Sequoyah symbols are embellished with a sort of pointillism.

August 1, 1874

Ani:tsa is dead forever, of the "black yellow."[4]

"I prayed in the morning, and alone at night. I suppose that I will be saved. There we are going, all of us."

It has probably been twenty years since he became a Christian, and he was seventy or eighty years old.

This he was saying a great deal, all the time he was able to walk about: "I talked to sinners and I prayed for them, and now if I am not able to talk to them, if now my speaking-time is past, I am ready to go. All of you know how I walked here below."[5]

DI:LASGE:SGI REPORTS THE COMMEMORATION OF THE ASSASSINATION OF CHIEF LINCOLN (1876)

While representing the Eastern Band in Washington on tribal business, an Indian named Di:lasge:sgi wrote to someone back home, perhaps a relative, of an event that impressed him—a vast and noisy commemoration of the assassination of a Great White Chief, eleven years after its occurrence. Di:lasge:sgi reported with the detachment that was perhaps proper for one who eleven years previously had fought to the end for another Great White Chief, one named Jefferson Davis.

April 15, 1876

Now! This is a small interesting thing that I tell all of you. On April 14th soldiers came here to town. They were marching in the streets, and the government of the white people recessed. Truly many thousands of people gathered. One could hear the sound of guns.

One said, "The reason is, Chief Lincoln died on April 14th."[1]

---

[4] In Cherokee semeiology a condition that might roughly equate with a grave circulatory disorder (see James Mooney and Frans M. Olbrechts, *The Swimmer Manuscript*, 224).

[5] MS in "The Inoli Letters."

[1] One recalls that Lincoln was wounded on April 14 and that he died the next day.

There are six of us Indians: two live in the North; one lives in the West; two of us are from North Carolina.²

Tse:gi Da:hw(a)sini, Ge:di A:yi:yv:ha, E:gi—I suppose that you all are getting along well. All of you must send me a letter.

I am well. De:wi Ada:ga and I, Di:lasge:sgi, are getting along well. We will stay here longer, perhaps.

[*on verso*]

This is Tse:gi's letter. I:no:li, you must read it to him and Timi.³

GANE:NU:LI:SGI RESIGNS AS SOLICITOR OF GOINGSNAKE DISTRICT (1877)

A hint of the hopelessness of the never ending struggle to prevent greedy whites from moving into the Cherokee Nation and pre-empting land is obtained from this letter of resignation, cast in Cherokee of rare elegance, to Principal Chief Charles Thompson (ca. 1821–1891) from the solicitor[1] of Goingsnake District. The new law which Solicitor Gane:nu:li:sgi found so difficult to interpret was probably the muddled edict concerning Cherokee citizenship that the Commissioner of Indian Affairs handed down on December 8, 1876.²

Goingsnake District³
Cherokee Nation
March 9, 1877

Now! Friend Utsale:dv,⁴ I just wrote you a few lines today.

[2] These must have been members of several different tribal delegations. We get a total of five individuals, not six.

[3] MS in "The Inoli Letters."

[1] The office of district solicitor was similar to that of the present-day county attorney in Oklahoma.

[2] See Morris L. Wardell, *A Political History of the Cherokee Nation*, 267–68.

[3] Goingsnake District, east of the national capital, Tahlequah, and lying against the Arkansas state line, was named for Goingsnake (sometimes spelled Going Snake) who was a Cherokee leader at the period of the Creek War, and later. The correct translation is "The Snakes Go (from here to there)"; the Cherokee form of the district named for him is I:nadanaí:yi.

[4] "Lichen," Thompson's Cherokee name.

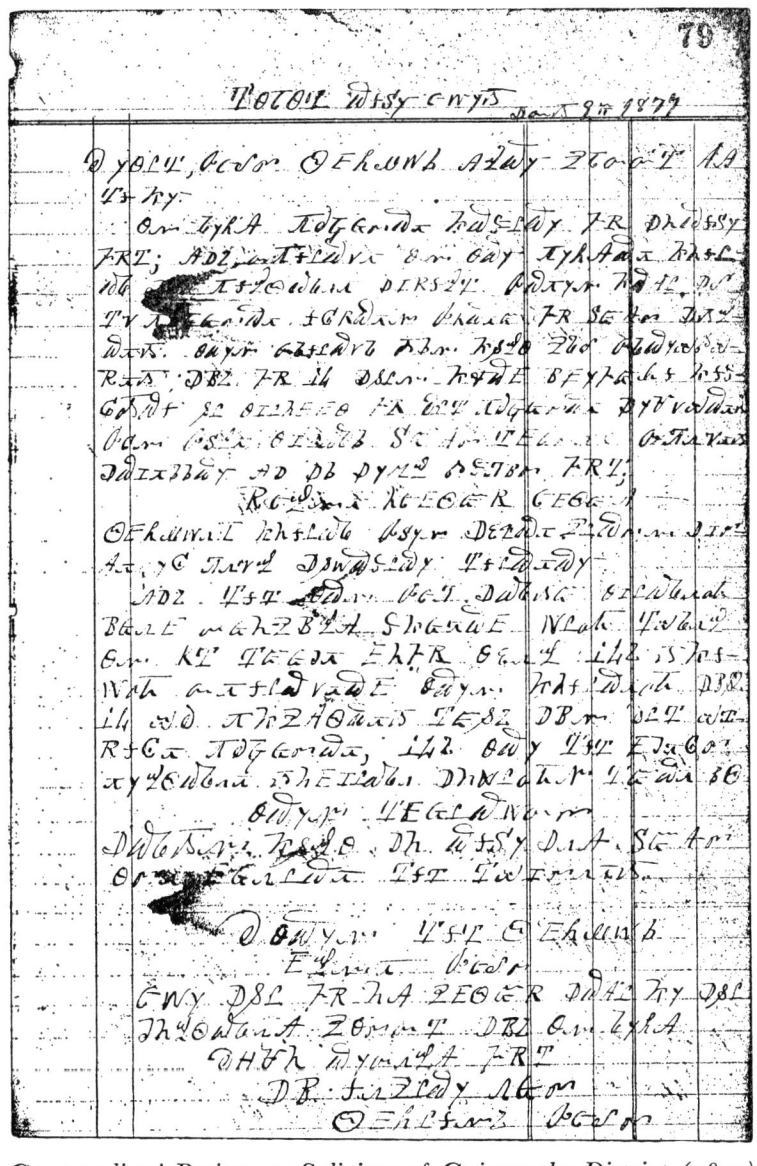

Gane:nu:li:sgi Resigns as Solicitor of Goingsnake District (1877)

Now I have just relinquished the District Solicitorship, and now this is why it has just come about: My head is simply too small for official work, and the new law is very difficult to interpret rightly. That is the reason why I have decided that it would be good to get a replacement.

Personally I do not desire to keep the job just because of the salary. I know my capabilities in enforcing the law. It has become desirable to do the right thing, and to ask someone to finish out my unfinished year.

Beloved Principal Chief, since it has become necessary to write you, I will be greatly hoping to hear that you have asked someone to become Solicitor. All of this has become very difficult, finding the . . .[5] homes of white intruders. Now I have made it known three times, and we do not know the reason why it has become this way. For I do not have the authority to remove them firmly in my hand, and I cannot continue to do the work of two persons. Since it has become difficult, I have just decided that those who live here in the District should think that I have done right.[6]

Now! That is all that I just wrote you, beloved Utsale:dv, Principal Head of the Cherokee Nation, and officials at the National capital.

I now relinquish the commission that you bestowed upon me.

I, Gane:nu:li:sgi Ne:wadv

I greet you, Utsale:dv.[7]

There is a notation upon this document to the effect that Principal Chief Thompson accepted the resignation upon March 22, 1877.

Ezekiel ("Zeke") Proctor Crusades for Good Government (1877)

The apathy of the present-day man on the street toward the

---

[5] This word is indecipherable.
[6] In resigning.
[7] MS in Cherokee Nation Papers.

stewardship of public servants has engendered strictures the size (and sometimes intrinsic interest) of a metropolitan telephone directory. It is refreshing, therefore, to discover that slipshod or corrupt officialdom did not pass inspection at the grassroots level in the old Cherokee Nation.

The fact that Ezekiel ("Zeke") Proctor of Goingsnake District was possibly the most dangerous and certainly the most slippery outlaw that ever troubled the peace of the Cherokee Nation may have no connection with the fact that the name in English of the aroused citizen who wrote this letter was Ezekiel ("Zeke") Proctor. Whether or not the two were one and the same individual is beside the point: a principle is a principle.

> August 25, 1877
> Goingsnake District,
> Cherokee Nation

Now! Now I will write you a few words about the way things happened to the one you made Sheriff,[1] Tsulio:wa of Tahlequah District.[2]

The United States Marshal[3] said that the grand jury had reindicted him. Sagho:nige is telling that this is true. They tried to get him out from where he is.[4] One hears that they are going to bring him to trial—perhaps on [August?] 27, 1877.

I am making a request of you, asking you which law you will use to remove him. Choose either of these two: U:hno:gv's

---

[1] Probably the high sheriff of the Cherokee Nation, warden of the National Jail in Tahlequah.

[2] Tahlequah (Dali:gwa) District, lying in the south-central part of the Cherokee Nation, contained the national capital which had the same name. For a discussion of the etymology of the place name "Tahlequah" see Jack Frederick Kilpatrick, "An Etymological Note on the Tribal Name of the Cherokees," *Journal* of the Graduate Research Center, Southern Methodist University, Vol. 30, No. 1 (Dallas, 1962), 40.

[3] Of the United States Court, Western District of Arkansas, presided over by the renowned "Hanging Judge," Isaac C. Parker (see Glenn Shirley, *Law West of Fort Smith, passim*).

[4] An attempted jail delivery by friends?

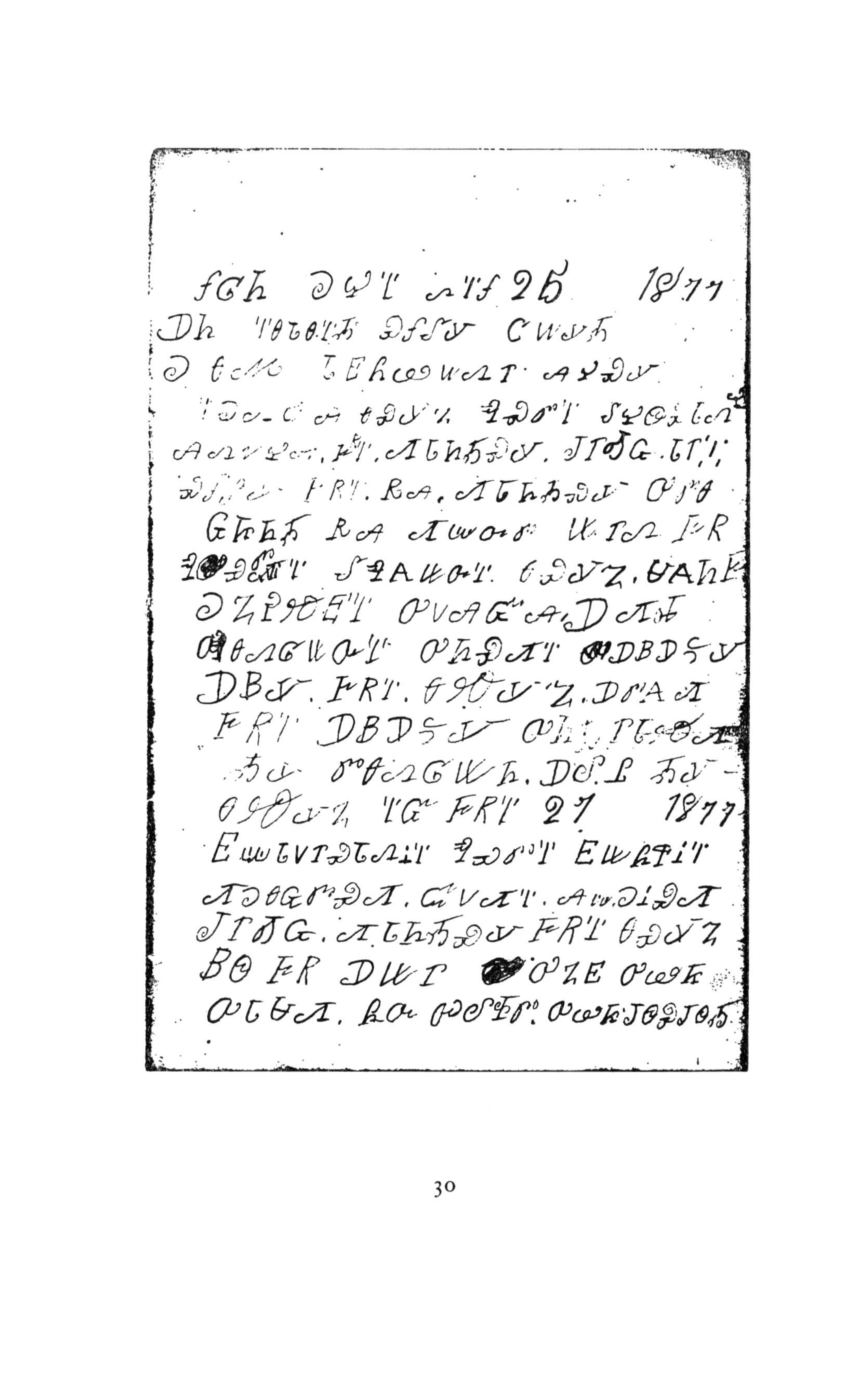

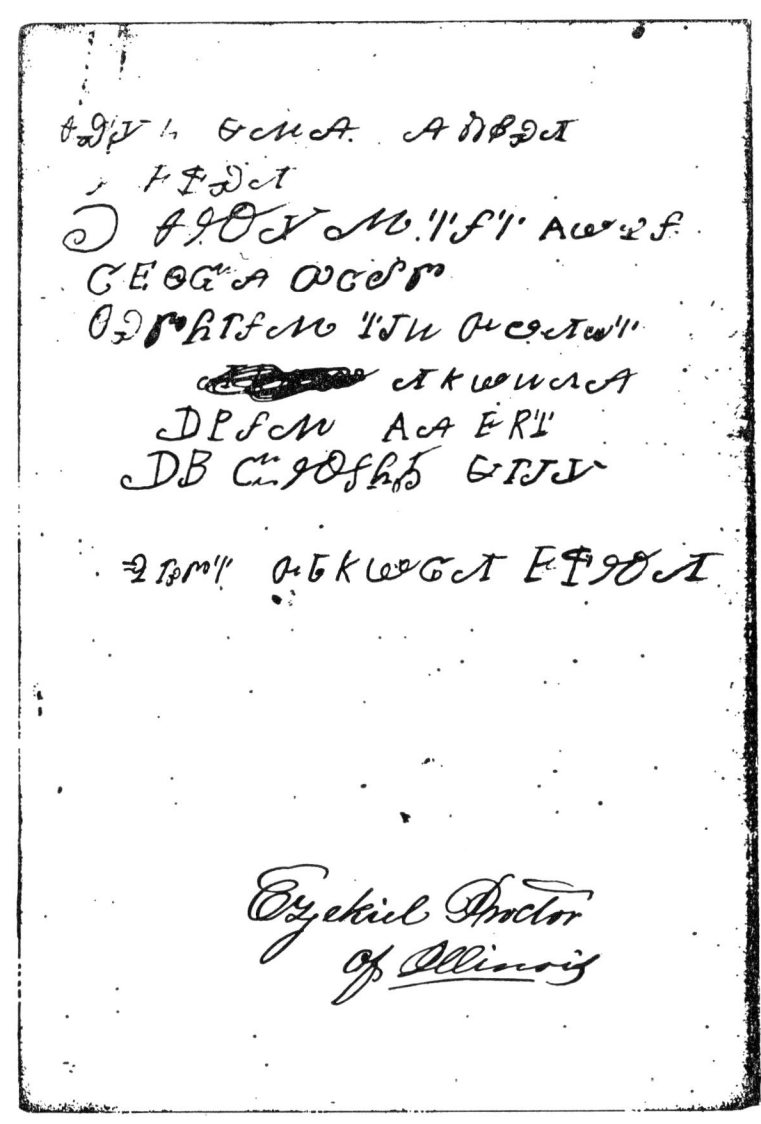

Ezekiel ("Zeke") Proctor Crusades for Good Government (1877)

son, or Uwe:da:sadh(i) Yo:nv, Ule:so:dv's son from Cooweescoowee District.⁵

Now! That is all that I just wrote Chief Utsale:dv.⁶ I greet both⁷ of you. Your writer with the medicine⁸ has just put the paper down.

I, Tsv:sgayo:o Sali:gug(i)

You must write me how it is.⁹

Methodist Revival Notice (1878)

From what little written evidence that has survived, one infers that Cherokee revival meetings of the last century varied but little from those of the rural whites. From what we know of Cherokee character, the difference must have lain chiefly in the greater emotional restraint displayed in the proceedings and a closer inspection by the sinners present of the rhetoric and amorous inclinations, if any, of the evangelist.

The notice here proves that the Methodists of Wolftown were not content merely to repel sin from their citadel of Echota Mission, but firmly financed to the extent of $3.25, were prepared to carry the campaign into other townships.

On this 14th day of September, 1878, they have begun. They will preach at Raven-place¹ for four days. Here in Painttown² brush arbor they will preach for four days, beginning on the 27th day of September.

⁵ Cooweescoowee, lying in the northwest corner of the Cherokee Nation, was by far the largest of the districts. Cooweescoowee (Guwi:sguwi) was the name of Principal Chief John Ross (1790–1866). Its exact meaning is no longer known, but it is said to be the term for some large white (perhaps aquatic) bird, either always rare, now extinct, or mythic (see Lester Hargrett, *Oklahoma Imprints, 1835–1890*, 18n.).

⁶ Principal Chief Charles Thompson, recipient of the letter (see n. 4, "Gane:nu:li:sgi Resigns as Solicitor of Goingsnake District [1877]").

⁷ The recipient and his wife?

⁸ Proctor the outlaw was a medicine man. The authors possess one of his conjuring books.

⁹ What steps were taken. MS in Cherokee Nation Papers.

¹ Raven-place (Gho:lanv̄:yi) is a general term for the southern part of Big Cove Township.

² A township adjacent to Wolftown on the west.

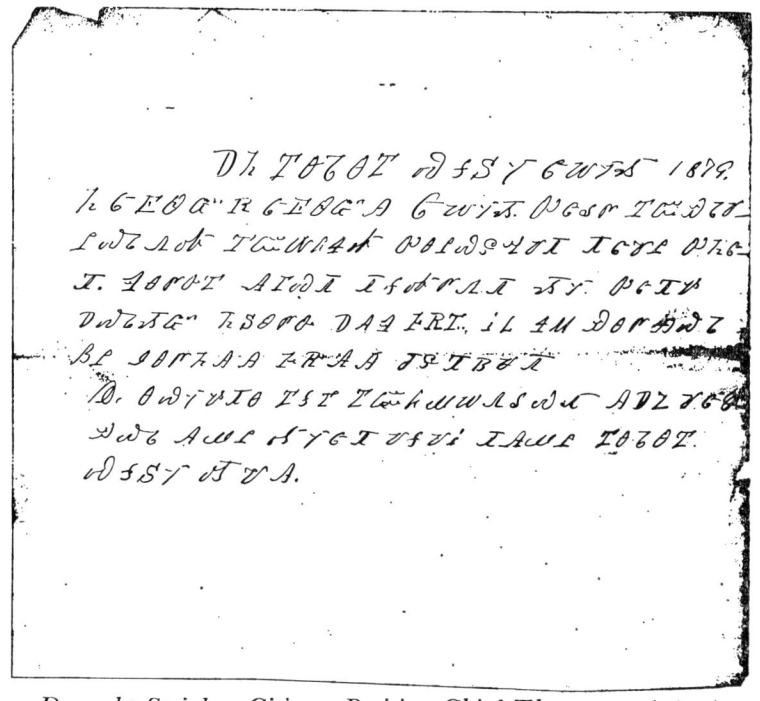

Drought-Stricken Citizens Petition Chief Thompson (1879)

[on verso]
Here at Echota they donated $3.25.[3]

Drought-Stricken Citizens Petition Chief Thompson (1879)

During the incumbency of Charles Thompson (Utsale:dv) as principal chief (1875–79) there were distressing crop failures in the Cherokee Nation. There exists a letter which presents us with a picture of this fullblood chief executive himself shrewdly haggling over the sale of a small quantity of corn in his possession.[1]

[3] MS in "The Inoli Letters."
[1] MS in Cherokee Nation Papers, translated by Jack Frederick and Anna Gritts Kilpatrick (scheduled for publication in *Chronicles of Oklahoma* with title "Letters in Cherokee of Chief Charles Thompson").

That corn[2] in the late 1870's still played its traditional role as the Cherokee staff of life is attested to by the following document, a petition for tribal aid from a group of drought-ruined citizens of Goingsnake District.

Here in Goingsnake District, Cherokee Nation, 1879 Principal Chief of the Cherokee Nation Utsale:dv, we pray to you and ask you for something to help your people. They have said that if you can do something for them, they are in need because they have not been able to raise any corn this year.[3]

Now! That is all that we have written you about what we in Goingsnake District met to do.[4]

[Here there follows a list of twenty-five signatures.][5]

Tso:wa Hungers for Election News (1881)

The intense interest which elections in the Cherokee Nation sometimes created may be inferred from this letter from Canadian District, in the southwest corner of the Nation, to a relative in Tahlequah District. There was a burning issue in the National Council election of 1881—the question concerning whether former slaves should share in the distribution of tribal funds. There was heavy pressure of the freedmen's organization and the United States government to force the Cherokees to accord freedmen full rights of Cherokee citizenship. A stubborn resistance took the position that the status of the former

---

[2] As late as ca. 1935 the Oklahoma Cherokees to some extent still grew a low-yield, colored strain of corn, no doubt aboriginal, that in palatability bore to the commercial corn of today approximately the same relationship as that of *pompano en papillote* to a can of sardines. There may be farmers with epicurean inclinations who, despite the blandishments of county farm agents, persist in growing this incomparable grain.

[3] This sentence is fully as faulty in Cherokee as it is in English.

[4] To prepare and present a petition.

[5] MS in Cherokee Nation Papers. There is a notation in English (by Chief Thompson, giving an instruction to a secretary?) upon this document: "Lewis Beamer Translate Those names in merican Languige."

slaves should be analogous to that of intermarried whites who were debarred from sharing in tribal moneys.[1]

Canadian District
Cherokee Nation
August 29, 1881

Now! Beloved Gho:ga Unedo:lv, I just wrote a few lines for you to read for this reason—I want to find out what happened in the election of National Councilmen in the other eight districts—if Tsunulv:hv:sgi's[2] forces won, or if they lost. I want you to tell me fully. I am asking you to send me a letter quickly. For tribal purposes I want to hear all that you know about the way that they voted, and I also want to hear what the leaders in various towns all around know. I also want to find out how all of you voted in Tahlequah District, and also in Flint District, where I came from.

They [the writer's faction] won here in Canadian District of the Cherokee Nation. They [the opposition] have given up all of them [the seats] in the lower house, and one in the upper house. It was truly very good!

There are not enough "black ones."[3] It will be all right in the upper house, and now in the lower house of the Nation they have given it all to us.

Now! Do everything you can to send me a letter for the purpose of telling me the way things are in the Cherokee Nation.

Now! That is all, I suppose. This is all I want—I want to hear from my relatives.

Now! That is all I just wrote.

I, Tso:wa Gan(i)si:ni U:ne:sdala

All are well this morning, and all are well around here.[4]

[1] See Wardell, *A Political History*, 222–40.

[2] "One Who Fails," the Cherokee name of Dennis Wolfe Bushyhead, principal chief, 1879–87. He may have been named for the distinguished North Carolina chief whose name, corrupted by the whites to Junaluska, is perpetuated in various geographical aspects of his native state. Junaluska died at an advanced age about 1858 (Mooney, *Myths of the Cherokee*, 164).

[3] The pro-freedmen faction.   [4] MS in collection of authors.

THE SHADOW OF SEQUOYAH

A Methodist Minister Dies as an Earthquake Is Born (1882)

Any extraordinary circumstances attending the passing of an individual are likely to be recorded not only in the necrology of that individual's family, but also in the notebooks of friends and neighbors who are somewhat given to interpreting those circumstances in the dim half-light of the old Cherokee religion and rural white superstition. In eastern Oklahoma, where seismic phenomena are all but unknown, the departure of a minister of the Gospel to the accompaniment of a genuine earthquake would be an event certain to set off a flurry of scribbling and speculation.

The earth shook on the 11th day of 1882[1] at 12 o'clock noon. Something amazing happened on this day. E:sigi passed from this earthly life at this time. He was a Methodist preacher.

"Now I finished all the work I was to do here on earth where I preached. Now I am going Above, to my Father's Place," he stated.

Just as he finished saying this, the earth shook.[2]

Former Clerk I:no:li Looks Up Death Records (1884)

It is evident that the clerk of Wolftown carefully recorded vital statistics, probably in a ledger that has not been preserved. This letter, very likely to someone at Cheowa, appears to be in reply to a request to look up the exact dates of the deaths of a pair of individuals, no doubt relatives of the one who made the request, some sixteen years previously.

Having been superseded by the Eastern Band government established in 1870, there was no township organization in Wolftown in 1884, but former Clerk I:no:li must have had the old township records in his possession. I:no:li himself died on July 5 of the year following that in which this letter was written.[1]

[1] January 11, in other words.
[2] MS in collection of authors.
[1] Gadigwanasdi, "Original Formulae in Cherokee Syllabary from the Gadigwanasti (Belt) Manuscript," MS.

It just became necessary for me to write about the year 1868. Now on July 13, 1884, I just wrote you.

I wrote on September 22, 1868, that Tse:gwadi:hi died on September 17th, and that Tsu:hla's mother, the widow of Ge:hida Uni:nidu:yv, died on the night of September 18th.

Tsa:ts(i) asked me to write a few words for you, Salo:li, to hear that Tsa:ts(i) is well and that Da:gi is well and that I, I:no:li, am getting along well.

Now! That is all. I, I:no:li, greet you and Sali:ni Ghiyu:ga both.

[on verso]

Salo:li Utsv:da Ghiyu:ga's letter.[2]

A:L(I)SA WRITES TO HER SHIFTLESS HUSBAND (ca. 1885)

We cannot be certain of the exact date of the penning of this revealing testimony to domestic infelicity at Qualla, but since I:no:li was asked to read it to his son Tso:saya[1] (who must have been illiterate) by the wrathful writer, the wife of his son, it might have been written as late as in the spring of 1885, the year of I:no:li's death.

Evidently Tso:saya had made some idle threat against his estranged wife, for with highly contrived sarcasm she points out that she has nothing to fear from her shiftless husband's gun, since he had lost it in pawn, but marriage to such an individual as he might well prove fatal! In the same vein she derides his intentions and abilities as a provider. She then defies him to do his legal worst.

But there is a surprise ending. With an abrupt modulation into the major key, she throws open the door for his return to conjugal bliss on the condition that he make token atonement by hoeing the corn that she has already gone to the trouble to plant for him!

Tso:saya!

[2] MS in "The Inoli Letters."
[1] Tso:saya's death on January 11, 1916 is recorded (not in a daily entry) in Will West Long, "Diary, September 20, 1913–August 17, 1914," MS.

Now! Now I just sent you a letter.

You have been bothering me. I, A:l(i)sa, have just heard something that you said—but the gun you pawned one can't get back, and it is evident that if I die, the reason will be because I am married to you!

When we first talked, you were to come here,[2] you said. That was all right, I thought. Now after all this time we are still looking for property.[3] We will have property, since you are looking for it so much! (I, too, am looking for property to own somewhere!)

It is all over. I suppose we will separate, since you are not helping us,[4] and you are not working, raising corn.

And this I hear from I:no:li, that you are going to take me into court.[5] I am not afraid of you, since I am an old woman.[6] You all don't know of any wrong that I did. You know one shouldn't tell a lie. You must tell the truth: you are a preacher.[7]

If you do take me into court, the white people will witness for me.[8] I am not afraid of you. Our children are liars[9]; that's the reason why you think you are going to take me into court.

If you will work good in our fields, I will be satisfied. For now I have finished planting corn; hoeing is all that it needs.

Now! That is all that I, A:l(i)sa, just wrote for you, Tso:saya, to hear.

---

[2] It would be customary for the husband after marriage to go to live with his wife's clanspeople. Apparently Tso:saya had gone back to his parental home.

[3] The word *tsugv:wahl(o)di* is difficult to translate: it can mean real estate, household goods, a grubstake, or wealth, among other things.

[4] The wife and children.

[5] It is not clear whether a tribal tribunal or a local white court is meant.

[6] "Mature woman," or "grown woman" might be a better translation.

[7] This might be an aside to I:no:li, who was to do the actual reading of the letter. I:no:li was a preacher; but, of course, his son, too, may have been a preacher.

[8] Perhaps A:l(i)sa lived near a reservation boundary and had white neighbors.

[9] Evidently Tso:saya was counting upon, or A:l(i)sa suspected that he was counting upon, the testimony of his children to prove maternal misconduct.

[*on verso*]
Yours, Tso:saya, for I:no:li to read.[10]

RECORD OF BORROWINGS FROM THE TREASURY OF THE EASTERN BAND (1885)

There exists a document[1] wherefrom one may learn that the Town Council of Wolftown in 1852 set interest rates for borrowers from the township treasury at 20 per cent for four months, 10 per cent for twelve months. Apparently after the setting up of a government for the whole Eastern Band, the tribe itself went into the moneylending business.

The document here appears to consist of file copies of notes given by the tribal treasurer to borrowers. Interest rates are not specified, but we wonder if they were not approximately the same as those which once permitted the city fathers of Wolftown to boast of a tidy $124.03 reposing in the township treasury.[2]

1885

You are to know by this letter, Ali:sini, that you owe $13.14 to the tribal authorities. The transaction took place July 10th.

For the cow[3] that was given you, Gho:gv, you owe $7.00 in all. The transaction took place July 10th.

To assist you, Nv:gi, you owe $16.50. The transaction took place July 11th.

[10] MS in James Mooney, Letters in "Cherokee Syllabary by Native Writers, 1887–92," MS No. 2241-b, American Bureau of Ethnology. The date in this file caption cannot be correct inasmuch as I:no:li, who was alive when the above letter was written, died in 1885, as shown by a notation on a MS in the archives of the Bureau of American Ethnology (see "Former Clerk I:no:li Looks Up Death Records [1884]").

[1] Translated in Kilpatrick and Kilpatrick, "Chronicles of Wolftown," Doc. 3.

[2] *Ibid.*

[3] We read that after W. C. McCarthy was appointed agent for the Eastern Cherokees in June, 1875, "a distribution was made of stock animals" (Mooney, *Myths of the Cherokee*, 174). This cow may have been a government animal given to the tribe, which thriftily sold it to an individual and retained the proceeds for the tribal treasury.

You owe $.30, Tsugh(a)dha:sdi Dhalu:gi:sgi. The transaction took place July 10th.[4]

A Medicine Man and a Minister Write to a Scientist (1888)

In the archives of the Bureau of American Ethnology, housed in one of the red towers of that architectural indiscretion, the main building of the Smithsonian Institution in Washington, repose two short letters that boast claims to singularity: they are to an ethnographer in the language of the American Indian tribe that he was studying at the time the letters were written; one of the missives is from a shaman, the other from a Baptist preacher.

No ethnologist was ever accepted by the Cherokees as was James Mooney of the Bureau of American Ethnology. His first visit to Qualla in 1887 was the beginning of a love affair with the Cherokee people that has endured beyond the grave. We remember asking an aged member of the Eastern Band, some thirty years after Mooney's death in 1921, if he had ever heard of the scientist. The sound of that name put fire in his old eyes. "Heard of him? I *knew* him!" he stated, with a lift of the chin.

One of the landmarks of Cherokee research is the translation and exegesis, left incomplete at Mooney's death and finished by Frans M. Olbrechts, of a notebook of the medicine man A:hyv́i:ní (ca. 1835–99), known to the whites as Swimmer.[1] From 1887 until his death Swimmer was Mooney's chief informant, and it was he who supplied the bulk of Mooney's great collection of Cherokee myths.[2]

The first of the two letters referred to is a hurriedly scrawled note from Swimmer to Mooney, evidently written in 1888, although in his haste the writer omitted the final numeral in the date. The "magistral" quality that Olbrechts[3] professed to observe in Swimmer's calligraphy is little evi-

[4] MS in "The Inoli Letters."
[1] Mooney and Olbrechts, *The Swimmer Manuscript*.
[2] Mooney, *Myths of the Cherokee*.
[3] Mooney and Olbrechts, *The Swimmer Manuscript*, 3.

denced in the jumble of scribbles. The medicine man had possibly been called away on a professional duty and had left this note behind at home to explain his failure to keep an appointment. The dollar referred to was, we suspect, in payment for past services as an informant. If it seems to be somewhat less than munificent as recompense, one must remember that at Qualla in 1888 thirty cents was considered to be a fair daily wage.

188[8?]

Now! Nv:do,[4] my friend, you and A:hyv́i:ní cannot see each other now. I have gone off to visit. You must talk with someone else until I return.

Give my child U:sguni the money, one dollar. I gave her permission to use it for something.

My friend Mu:ni,[5] I, A:hyv́i:ní, just wrote this on August 6th.

(Tsa:ladi:hi,[6] you must read this letter for him.)

Mooney first made his home at Qualla with Su:ye:dv U:gu:ghu, a native minister of gigantic size who had been chief of the Eastern Band and a lieutenant in the Thomas Legion. He was a highly skilled carpenter, mason, and blacksmith.[7] Su:ye:dv wrote the following letter to Mooney in Washington to where the scientist had returned after his field work in 1877, sending it to Chief Smith at the St. Charles Hotel on Pennsylvania Avenue where Smith was staying while upon tribal business in the national capital. Smith no doubt interpreted the missive for Mooney.

[4] *Nv:do sv:no:yi é:hi* ("the major heavenly body that belongs to the night") is the Cherokee designation for moon. The shortened form, Nv:do, was bestowed upon Mooney for an obvious reason.

[5] A direct spelling of Mooney with Sequoyah symbols, one of them the rarely employed *mu*.

[6] The Cherokee equivalent of Jarrett. The individual referred to here was Nimrod Jarrett Smith (ca. 1836-93), chief of the Eastern Band at the time of this letter.

[7] Sv:ye:dv U:gu:ghu means "The-Chosen-One Hoot-owl." This information was obtained in a conversation with his grandson, Mr. George Owl, in March, 1963.

May 22, 1888
Swaney,[8] North Carolina
Cherokee Post Office

I, Su:ye:dv U:gu:ghu, just wrote this for you, my dear friend Nv:do, to read. I assume you are getting along well. I have hope of finding you well and of your doing for me what I am writing about.

I am happy that you gave me so much support. It is evident that you love ministers of the Baptist Church.[9] And that is not all: the Ruler who lives above feels good.

This is all that I will write.

If you should change,[10] tell your friends plainly, if you can, that it is quite true that I have very little wealth to support my family while I go about preaching to various congregations. Ask them up in Washington to think of me.

Now, dear Nv:do, I am going to stop writing. Send me a letter quickly, if you can. I send you my greetings.[11]

A MEDICINE MAN'S SON FAILS TO FIND HIDDEN PAPERS (1888)

Another informant of James Mooney in the late 1880's was Da:gwadi:hi, a medicine man who died not long thereafter at the age of seventy. This native doctor was not literate in the Sequoyah syllabary, and the conjurations that Mooney obtained from him were taken down by a son.[1] Da:gwadi:hi also supplied Mooney with a store of myths.[2]

---

[8] Big Cove.

[9] Mooney, who was a Roman Catholic, must have given Su:ye:dv financial assistance out of his own pocket. Certainly much of Mooney's extraordinary success as an ethnographer derived from his sympathy and tact.

[10] Perhaps Mooney had mentioned some tentative plan to accept a new position.

[11] MSS in Mooney, "Letters in Cherokee Syllabary by Native Writers, 1887–1892."

[1] Mooney, "Sacred Formulas of the Cherokees," 316–17. These are found in Mooney, "259 Cherokee Text (Sacred?) Formulas," MS, *passim*. No study of them has yet been made.

[2] Mooney, *Myths of the Cherokee, passim*. There is a photograph of the medicine man, p. 256.

Social Documents of the Cherokees, 1862–1964

The letter translated here is the record of Mooney's attempt to locate and obtain from Da:gwadi:hi medical writings that were at the home of a son, perhaps the one referred to above, who lived at Cheowa. (Incidentally, the meaning of this geographical term—Tsiyo:hi in Cherokee—is "Otter-place.")

Da:gwadi:hi may not have been able to read, but he knew how to treasure his manuscript medical library. Sympathy with the tribulations of the son comes easily to anyone who has had experience with the habits of medicine men. With much cunning they hide their arcana in the rafters of their cabins, in barns, smokehouses, nearby crevices and caves, and in jars buried in the ground.

Cheowa, North Carolina
Robbinsville, N. C.
Oct. 4, 1888

Now! Da: gwadi:hi, my father, I hope that this letter finds you well. We are all well here.

Now! This is the way it is about the medical papers for which you were asking: I did not find them. These are all that I found—two kinds. It was not easy to find them; it was difficult. Now it is time for the one who will take them for me to leave. This flint[3] spoken of I can't find. What I am sending you is all that I found. That is all that I can do. It is difficult to read these papers. Later on they can be found.

It is difficult to think this week because I don't have the time. The reason is, I have to work. Don't let him[4] make a hasty decision about what I have sent you. I suppose I can't find the papers that you wanted in a hurry. You find them yourself, whenever you have time.

That is all that I, Tsa:ni Da:gwadi:hi, just wrote for you, my father, to hear.[5]

---

[3] A piece of flint was used as an implement for surgery and for ceremonial scarification. See Mooney and Olbrechts, *The Swimmer Manuscript*, 68–71.

[4] James Mooney.

[5] MS in Mooney, "Letters in Cherokee Syllabary by Native Writers, 1887–1892."

The Heirs of De:nili o:hla Write to the Judge of Flint District (1891)

Flint (Dawi:sgalv́:yi), the smallest and geographically ruggedest of the districts of the Cherokee Nation, lay directly south of Goingsnake District along the Arkansas state line. Most of it is now in Adair County. It was named for the exceeding abundance of broken, sharp chert that still makes its backroads a terror to tires.

Records of the voluminous litigation that clogged the district courts for some three-quarters of a century have disappeared except for a few remnants such as this, found in a ledger containing some records of Echota Baptist Church which stands in the valley of Hummingbird Branch in western Adair County. There is a local legend in the Echota community that Judge Dv́:n(a)dé:dhon(i), an Echotan, was a Baptist minister as well as a political figure, and that he named the church at Echota for New Echota, the capital of the old Cherokee Nation in Georgia. Echotans, who speak a distinct dialect of Cherokee, believe themselves to be the descendants of the people who once lived in and about New Echota.

> Here in Flint District, Cherokee Nation,
> January 4, 1891

Beloved Judge Dv́:n(a)dé:dhon(i) of Flint District:

We bring this before you and petition you.

This is the way it is: We are the heirs to the property of the late De:nili O:hla. He lived in Flint District. We are now asking you to do what is written in the Constitution—to appoint appraisers. Appoint Du:si Gha:n(a)sgawi as executor of this estate.

Here below we just wrote our names.

> Ge:hyahi
> Ne:ni
> Adi:dhlidó:hi Hi:yiné:i
> Ne:ni Hi:yiné:i

The late De:nili O:hla and we had the same mother. We are the last living survivors, second in line,[1] and heirs.

You Beloved One![2]

Di:dagw(i) Writes of His Illness (1893)

The following curious letter, so full of *Weltschmerz*, in the original Cherokee is cast, appropriately enough, in the format of a formal funeral notice. The writer does not specify which disease destroyed the friends and the friendship that he mourns, and which he feels will carry him off, too, but we suspect that an epidemic was raging in Tahlequah District in 1893.

1893

Here in Tahlequah District it was March 12th, this year that we, Da:gwadi:hi Digv:wa:sade:sgi, became friends—and all our brothers, sisters, and in-laws loved each other—I and Sa:mi Ga?ni.

And all about I had friends, and it is very sad that there is sickness. I suppose that we are all going.

I have that sickness.

That is all that I just wrote for you, Da:gwadi:hi, to read.

I, Di:dagw(i).[1]

Charm for Assistance in War (1894)

The Cherokees see no inconsistency in their vivid self-image as a peace-loving people and the fact that throughout their recorded history they have gone to war with foreseeable regularity. In this respect they resemble the general populace of the United States.

While in Cherokee culture there are few survivals of institutionalized militarism, there exists an appreciable number of charms for protection and success in battle. Most of these, appropriate to emergency conditions where much ritual is

---

[1] Not direct descendants.
[2] MS in collection of authors.
[1] MS in collection of authors.

impossible, are quite short, and are merely to be said. Some of them prescribe the adjunctive expectorating upon the hands and the symbolic washing of the face, and perhaps body, with saliva.[1]

The example below is from eastern Cherokee County, Oklahoma.

May 9, 1894[2]

Now! Blue Thunder,[3] very quickly You have just come to make a home.
Now You have just come to join the body.[4]
Now! Red Thunder![5]
Ha! You splattered blood!
(This written on paper is to help one in war.)[6]

The Judge of Goingsnake District Advises Reconciliation (1897)

Documents pertaining to loans seldom have much lilt, being apt to be weighted with need or greed, but the two reproduced here, found in a small trunk in Adair County, Oklahoma, record a transaction that, for all of its beginning in routine usury, took flight into beauty at the end.

The first document records a loan by a man to a woman. It is couched in Cherokee legal terminology which is obviously patterned upon that used by the whites, but which still maintains its own flavor:

---

[1] This washing with saliva, in Cherokee medico-religious theory the vital body fluid, and "Going to the Water" (see " 'Going to the Water' Prayer for Longevity [1930]") has an obvious relationship. For additional examples of battle charms for Oklahoma, see Jack Frederick Kilpatrick, *The Siquanid' Dil'tidegi Collection*, 5–6.

[2] Probably the date upon which the writer learned the charm.

[3] For the tutelary role of thunder, see Kilpatrick and Kilpatrick, *Friends of Thunder*, 50–56. In Cherokee color symbolism blue is the hue of disaster and failure. In other words, Thunder, the puissant protector of the Cherokees, turns his "blue" aspect toward the enemy.

[4] "You have just come to become a part of me."

[5] In his "red," or successful aspect, Thunder fights for his friends.

[6] MS in collection of authors.

CONTRACT

Goingsnake District, December 31, 1894

I have entered into contract with Digu:hl(e)di:sgi Wa:dh(i). He lent me $40.00, to be repaid in either one year or two years. The interest is to be $.10 upon each dollar. January 1, 1895, is the beginning date of the contract to repay into which I have entered.

Now this states my name which I just wrote,

E:lini Utsi:tsadh(a)

Witnesses:
U:daniyv:dv Tso?idi:h(i)
Tsa:wayu:ga Tso?idi:h(i)
Sawa:ni U:do:lanv:sdi

E:lini must have found it necessary to elect the two-year option, for Digu:hl(e)di:sgi had scrawled at the bottom of the document:

January 9, 1896

The interest on the $40.00 was paid.

At some time during the later life of the contract E:lini died without having fulfilled her obligation. We infer that Digu:hl(e)di:sgi threatened court action against the heirs, and that one of them, probably a daughter, much incensed, went to the judge of Goingsnake District for advice. This noble letter of the judge to the creditor breathes a spiritual elevation that is almost Biblical:

Here in Goingsnake District, Cherokee Nation
December 1, 1897

Now! Digu:hl(e)di:sgi Wa:dh(i), my friend, I will write a few words for you to read.

Today Ne:n(i)si Utsi:tsadh(a) came and asked what is to happen. You extended the late E:lini credit. We all knew—it was evident—that she had nothing. You lent her money, and now she is dead. Even if E:lini had left anything in the way of possessions, the law does not permit reparation. But Ne:n(i)si herself simply wants to feel right about it. Her soul is much troubled.

You two talk it over together. You two should just forgive each other. The way that you will have unburdened yourself will be exceedingly joyful. You should forgive her. Somewhere one will find that one can do that. You two make this right. Perhaps one can understand this sort of saying when one is dead forever.

Somewhere, somehow, you two should sincerely forgive each other. That is what she wants, and I want it, too. All I want is for you two to make this right.

Now! That is all that I have written.

Diga:sa:gwalv Di:ni:nv
Judge, Goingsnake District[1]

Conjuration for Muscular Cramps (1898)

There exist in manuscript a great many conjurations for the purpose of relieving muscular cramps and aches, in Cherokee medical theory commonly interpreted to be a complication of the condition known as the "black," which itself is held to be a subtype of the "yellow." One of these curing procedures, written in beautifully formed Sequoyan, bears the date December 14, 1898—the day, no doubt, that the medicine man from Se:lamí:yi, in southeastern Adair County, Oklahoma, either learned it from some colleague, or else just decided to commit it to writing.

> Now! Listen! Ha! Now the Wizards[1] have just come to let you[2] know that They have just eyed where the Important Thing[3] is resting.

---

[1] MSS in collection of authors.

[1] Cherokees cringe when they learn from the authority of the standard bibliographic source that their term for a medicine man is *ada:wé:hi*. An *ada:wé:hi* is a spirit or human being of transcendental power; therefore, it is as improper to refer to a journeyman medicine man, a *dida:hnvwi:sg(i)*, as an *ada:wé:hi* as it would be to address the minister of the corner church as "Seraph." The term *ada:wé:hi* is usually translated as "wizard."

[2] The patient.

The Wizards, from the Nightland where they are convening, have just come to empower Them[4] to cause the White[5] to take it away.

You Wizards! Ha! Now You have met everywhere in the Four Corners.[6]

You Wizards! Ha! Now You Two Appointed Ones[7] have just appeared.

You Two Wizards, command it![8]

Ha! You Two Wizards fail in nothing.

Ha! Now You Two come, appear where the Important Thing is resting!

You Two Wizards quickly raise him [or her][9] up!

You Two have just come to fill the Turtle Shell with the Important Thing.

Ha! Now, Important Thing! Ha! Now, Important Thing!

They will be helping him [or her] to step upon the treetops.

Ha! You Two will be carrying the Turtle Shell filled with the Important Thing.

When You Two carry it, take the Important Thing toward the Sunland, so that it will not turn back again.

Make the Important Thing impotent.

"Relief!" I will be saying.

His [or her] name——; his [or her] clan is——.

His [or her] soul will be rising again from the treetops.

(To doctor tendons: One lays down the white cloth; the turtle shell lies underneath the white cloth, which is on top. White beads are crossed over lengthwise, but if they are not available, threads, spaced out, are placed. One begins by doctor-

---

[3] A stylized circumlocution for the disease.

[4] The Two Appointed Ones.

[5] The propitiary white cloth (aboriginally deerskin), the *u:gi:sdi* ("to take, he [or she]").

[6] The four cardinal directions.

[7] The two Sons of Thunder.

[8] The Important Thing.

[9] The patient.

ing the chest, and then the back is likewise scratched[10] all over, using a green blackberry thorn from a thicket.)[11]

GHE:N(I)DI SV:GHI NECROLOGY (1900–1901)

Out of the painstaking plodding of any Cherokee document poetry is apt to whirr up and wing off, like a bird startled by heavy feet. Perhaps we are dealing with some sort of dichotomy in the very nature of Cherokees, who at one minute can be meticulously and mechanically hewing wood and drawing water, and at the next casting over their work the magic of dew and wood smoke.

These necrological jottings, as precise as they are tender, concern themselves, Cherokee-fashion, with exact chronometric particulars before they move off into a grave nobility, utterly devoid of sentimentality, yet pulsing with feeling.

The writer was a southeastern Adair County medicine man whose name, in its English form, Candy Mink, is perpetuated by a spring near his old home in the wilderness.

1.

On October 27, 1900, at eight minutes past 6 o'clock in the morning, the late Digo:hisdi:sgi Ga:gama finished his life, 19 years old. He was nearly 20; he lacked two months and four days of being 20 years old.

And now he has passed from the earth to the Place of Long Rest, leaving behind the anguish of living; now he has been healed of his pain.

I, Ghe:n(i)di Sv:ghi, just wrote this.

He began life January 1, 1881. The next January 1st he would have been 20 years old.

2.

On April 17, 1901, there finished his life on earth a boy, the late Tso:ni Sv:ghi. Seven years, five months, and two days is how long he lived in this tormented world, and now in the

---

[10] For ceremonial scratching, see Mooney and Olbrechts, *The Swimmer Manuscript*, 68–71.

[11] MS in collection of authors.

Do:yaní:si Asks Chief Buffington to Identify Him (1901)

Place of Long Rest he reposes. He was my beloved son. Already now he has left me, and with tears I, Ghe:n(i)di Sv:ghi, just wrote this.

It was 12 o'clock at night, 15 minutes toward morning, when his breathing told that he had become quiet, and then the end came.

Now! That is all that I, Ghe:n(i)di Sv:ghi, just wrote.[1]

Do:YANÍ:SI ASKS CHIEF BUFFINGTON TO IDENTIFY HIM (1901)

The Dawes Commission, named for its chairman, Henry L. Dawes, was created by the United States in 1893 for the purpose of extinguishing tribal title to land in Indian Territory in preparation for the statehood of what became Oklahoma. One of its duties was the enrollment of Indians and the allotment to them of individual holdings of land.[1]

Since many citizens of the Cherokee Nation were not living at home at the time of enrollment, numerous difficulties in identification arose. The Cherokee who, as we see here, took his problem directly to the principal chief, may have been an intermarried member of the Eastern Band.

Cherokee, North Carolina
August 17, 1901

Beloved Da:mi Ganvhi:da,[2] Principal Chief, Tahlequah, Indian Territory:

Now! I will write a few words.

A few days ago I saw that a letter that I sent had returned. "Send the Dawes Commission a letter," he told me. That I did. Again it returned, I saw.

You from the Tahlequah government, write to them, identifying me. Uhyalu:ga's mother knows about it, they told me. Then I sent a letter there, and I also saw a letter. I am glad that he has found my name written down on October 22, 1881.

---

[1] MS in collection of authors.
[1] Wardell, *A Political History*, 312–13.
[2] "Tom Long," T. M. Buffington.

What shall I do? Can you let me know fully? I want to find out now. It is strange.

I, Tsa:ni Do:yaní:si[3]

Address upon the Keetoowah Society (1901)

To our knowledge, no thorough study of the Cherokee organization known to the whites as the Keetoowah[1] Society has yet been published. It is said to have been founded in 1859 by the influential Baptist missionaries Evan and John Jones to perpetuate Christian ideals, Abolitionism, and certain aboriginal cultural values, and to have been superimposed upon a pre-existing organization of great antiquity.[2]

An outthrust of the Keetoowah Society was the nativistic "Nighthawk" movement[3] which under the leadership of Redbird Smith (Dhotsu:hwa Sighwani:da, 1850–1918) and his sons exercised from 1896 to ca. 1935 a powerful influence upon the conservative fullblood element. At present the Keetoowah Society still exists, but its force is weakened by schisms and blunted by the militant opposition of Cherokee Christians.

The following document, written with poor calligraphy and uncommonly erratic spelling upon a sheet of rough brown tablet paper, was in the effects of a Keetoowah Society official who died in the spring of 1962, although it is not his holograph.

October 3, 1901

I just wrote an address upon the way the Keetoowah is organized:

Now! In a few words I will make plain the way our Keetoowah is organized; for we do not have anything like the law of the Apportioner[4] that they have elsewhere.

This is what our Apportioner gave to us, the Indians: the

---

[3] MS in Cherokee Nation Papers.
[1] The etymology of this word, *Ani:gidu:hwagi*, stands in need of study.
[2] Wardell, *A Political History*, 121.
[3] See Thomas, "The Redbird Smith Movement," Bureau of American Ethnology *Bulletin 180* (1961), *passim*.
[4] *Une:hlanv:hi*, the Supreme Being.

53

White Pathway that leads to the House. Our Pathway, the White Pathway of the Apportioner, is all that there is to help us.[5] If we understand and believe in the Keetoowah, it sustains us forever.

This is the way it will be: If we do not listen, we cannot understand; if we do not listen, it will always be this way where we live. It will never be easy until we arrive There; it will be just as it is.[6]

But if we listen to our Apportioner when He speaks, all of us will be mingled together There; our own will arrive There.

It is difficult for the multitude to understand. In order to appeal to them, one has to speak much. Then they will learn what to do.

But they who do not take heed may think that elsewhere they will find help.

Now! That is all.[7]

Memorandum Concerning a Runaway Teen-Age Girl
(1902)

Some of the oddments in Cherokee family papers are indeed odd, but disquieting visions of some of our own attics will perhaps lay a restraining hand upon fingers groping for the first stone. This vignette of the turn of the century juvenile delinquency was treasured up in a small trunk in a cabin on Baron Fork of the Illinois River in northern Adair County.

I just wrote this on June 8, 1902, as an aid to remembering how it happened.

Sunday evening a 14-year-old girl ran away from home. All day Monday and all night Monday night I hunted her. On Tuesday morning, June 8th, I found her.

Dhlvdi:sd(a) came outside. He was saying, "I heard her say,

---

[5] One is tempted to translate this as "to save us." The stem—*sdel*—is consistently translated "save" in the New Testament.

[6] In other words, the material situation will be adverse.

[7] MS in collection of authors.

'Let's go to An(a)sde:gwo,' "[1] Dhlvdi:sd(a) came to say. "The girls have gone there now."

Then I spoke. "She just returned," I said. "She was the one that was responsible for it."[2]

SE:DÍ:HI FIRE OF THE KEETOOWAH SOCIETY COLLECTS FUNDS FOR FOOD (1906–1907)

From the original *gadhi:yo*[1] established at Redbird Smith's home in Illinois[2] District in 1902,[3] there sprang a network of what the Cherokees called "Fires" throughout the Cherokee Nation. At the height of the Redbird Smith movement there were approximately a score of these, each of which consisted of a highly developed organization in the vicinity of a centrally located *gadhi:yo*.

One of these Fires was that of Se:dí:hi,[4] in the neighborhood of what the whites called Long Prairie, in Goingsnake District. The ensuing translation is drawn from a small book made by the sewing together of loose sheets from a stationery tablet, a part of the records of the treasurer of Sedí:hi Fire. The contributions recorded, ranging in size (if one does not consider the fifth entry) from $.02 to $.50, were made for the purpose of assisting in catering Keetoowah meetings, involving several Fires, held upon a hill called Nv:ya Ghayv:sadv́:i[5] in the community now known to the whites as Stony Point, in central Adair County.

The names of the contributors, as we know from other documents in our possession, are those of men, women, and

[1] We cannot identify this place. It means "Big Sticks."
[2] MS in collection of authors.

[1] *Gadhi:yo*, *gadhiyó:hi*, and *gadhi:ya* are different forms of the name for the aboriginal townhouse. In Oklahoma a *gadhi:yo* is a central meeting-place, usually called by the white people, who unfailingly reduce everything Indian to its lowest spiritual connotation, a "stomp ground."
[2] The Cherokee name is Atsi:sgvhnagesdv́:yi ("Redhorse [a fish] Domain-place"). The name for the Illinois River is "Redhorse Domain."
[3] Thomas, "The Redbird Smith Movement," Bureau of American Ethnology *Bulletin 180* (1961), 164.
[4] "Walnut-place."
[5] "Stone Nose-place."

children. The size of the donations, the hints about the cuisine, and the custom of defraying the expenses of visiting delegations are of much interest.

TO BUY FOOD WITH

Ganvhidv́:yi,[6] December 6, 1906. For future expenses we, the Se:dí:hi Fire, collected money with which to buy coffee.

[Here there follows a list of fifteen individuals who contributed a total of $.74.]

Goingsnake District, January 16, 1907. There will be a meeting at Nv:ya Ghayv:sadv́:i. We, the Se:dí:hi Fire, collected money to buy a pig. The contributors are named here:

[Here there follows a list of nine individuals who contributed a total of $.45.]

At Nv:ya Ghayv:sadv́:i on April 6, 1907, there will be a meeting at which many will gather. Food, expense money, to buy flour, was collected by us, the Se:dí:hi Fire. The contributors are named here:

[Here there follows a list of seven individuals who contributed a total of $.57.]

For future expenses at Nv:ya Ghayv:sadv́:i on June 4, 1907, they, the Se:di:hi Fire, collected money with which to buy flour.

[Here there follows a list of six individuals who contributed a total of $.75.]

The Treasurer was paid by: Gwe:ni Digo:hw(a)dhi:sgi, the only one who paid $1.00 for coffee, Tsuna:walo:di, the only one who paid in full.

Ganvhidv́:yi, July 8, 1907. The Se:dí:hi Fire collected money for future expenses.

[Here there follows a list of nineteen individuals who contributed a total of $2.45.]

July 8, 1907. They contributed for coffee.

[Here there follows a list of four individuals who contributed a total of $.85.]

[6] "Long-place." Long Prairie.

To buy a pig for the meeting at Nv:ya Ghayv:sadv́:i on August 15, 1907, at which many will gather we, the Se:dí:hi Fire collected money here.

[Here there follows a list of fifteen individuals who contributed a total of $1.83.]

For the meeting at Nv:ya Ghayv:sadv́:i on August 15, 1907, at which many will gather, they were asked for money to buy a cow. $1.11 was obtained.

Money collected to aid the delegation of four that will visit those at Nv:ya Ghayv:sadv́:i on August 11, 1907:

[Here there follows a list of twenty-three individuals who contributed a total of $3.05.]

For the meeting at Nv:ya Ghayv:sadv́:i on October 26, 1907, at which many will gather we, the Se:dí:hi Fire, collected money to buy a cow.

[Here there follows a list of nineteen individuals who contributed a total of $3.54.]

This is to aid the delegation at Nv:ya Ghayv:sadv́:i on October 26, 1907:

[Here there follows a list of fifteen individuals who contributed a total of $2.11.][7]

"THE PANTHER AND THE CRANE"—
A NATCHEZ CHEROKEE MYTH (ca. 1908)

The tribal identity of the Natchez people perished in the war with the French that began in 1729, but Natchez blood still flows in the descendants of these Indians who escaped the slavery or the stake that was the lot of a large segment of their kinsmen by fleeing to the Creeks and the Cherokees. A small colony of Indians, of mixed Natchez, Cherokee, and Creek blood, lives about the southern end of Tenkiller Lake; up until a few years ago some of them could still speak Natchez.

During the period 1908–11 the ethnologist John R. Swanton collected myths[1] from these Natchez Cherokees. One of those

[7] MS in collection of authors.
[1] John R. Swanton, *Myths and Tales of the Southeastern Indians*. Bureau of American Ethnology *Bulletin 88* (1929).

tales, "The Panther and the Crane," told to him in Cherokee, he scribbled down in a phonetic system and deposited in the archives of the Bureau of American Ethnology. Curious concerning whether the version of "The Panther and the Crane" that appears in the collection of Southeastern Indian myths published by Swanton differed significantly in detail from that in his phonetic transcription, the present authors painfully deciphered Swanton's scrawl, transcribed it into Sequoyah syllabary, and retranslated the myth.

Small discrepancies indeed did appear; but something of greater moment stood forth—the spirit of Indian storytelling, direct and strong, in not the slightest need of literary polish.

The Panther and the Crane had a contest.
"Let's have a contest. Let's throw," the Panther was told [by the Crane].
He [the Panther] told the Crane, "Do it this way: let's throw a hammer."
"Let's throw it across [a stream]," they said.
The Panther threw first. He threw it across.
Then the Crane began. "I can't throw it across," he thought. He decided that it was too big.
("If one of us fails to throw it across, that one will be killed," they had said to each other [before the contest].)
He [the Crane] began to whistle.
"Why do you whistle?" he was asked.
"I think that this hammer will land over there where my older brother lives. I want him to hear. That's why I whistle. A blacksmith—that's what he used to call me."
"If that's the way it is, don't throw it. I use it myself."
He [the Crane] thought of something else.
"Let's have an eating contest," he told him [the Panther].
Then they ate.
The Crane had a bag attached to himself. When eating, he put it [the food] into the bag. The Panther didn't find it out. He kept on eating.

When they ate it [the food] all up, they put some more in [their dishes] and continued eating.

It became too much for the Panther. He died.

The Crane beat the Panther.²

VISION OF A CHRISTIAN CHILD (1908)

This strange document, written in pencil, was in a collection of papers from Nofire Hollow, in the extreme western part of Adair County, Oklahoma. Since all of these manuscripts had been written in the old Flint District, the little girl must have lived somewhere in that political division of the Cherokee Nation, but seemingly there is no way to determine who she was, for her name is a common one.

Tsígo:ne:la died on December 29, 1908. She was four years and eleven months.

It was quite interesting what she said when she was still well, about four months ago:

"Ú:galo:gá (her uncle) that they say died, did not die. He lives in God's Place. He and the angels sang to me," she said, "and it was as if he were preaching—the way he spoke and the way he was doing. He was waving his hands and his arms—and first he sang.

"This is what he was saying: 'Jesus Christ is standing at the Doorway. "Come in," He says.' "¹

A CHEROKEE CHRONOLOGY (ca. 1909)

Accompanying entries in a notebook largely given over to the brassy claims of a certain patent medicine show that the following brief chronology was written down about 1909 by a shaman who lived near Bunch, in southcentral Adair County, Oklahoma. The fact that the wrong years are assigned to certain events may be accepted as evidence that the chronology

² "The Panther and the Crane," MS in Bureau of American Ethnology. This story is not found in either of the major collections of Cherokee myths, Mooney, *Myths of the Cherokee*, and Kilpatrick and Kilpatrick, *Friends of Thunder*.

¹ MS in collection of authors.

was either based upon oral tradition, or else inaccurately copied from an older manuscript.

To find what happened long ago in the year:

The earth shook[1]	1811
The Creek War occurred[2]	1813
They surveyed the land in Georgia[3]	1828
Sequoyah first followed and found them[4]	1831
The stars fell[5]	1833
The people came out here[6]	1837
The people received money[7]	1851
The Government War occurred[8]	1861

MENU FOR A MEETING OF THE KEETOOWAH SOCIETY (1909)

This note to an official of the Se:dí:hi Fire of the Keetoowah Society by an official of the Nv:ya Ghayv:sadv́:i Fire advises the former of what his organization is expected to provide in the way of comestibles for a convocation at the *gadhi:yo* of the latter. The *pièce de résistance* is not specifically mentioned, but the clues to its identity are present in the words "soup" and "you squirrel hunters." *Salo:lu:gam(a)*, a soup or stew made of young squirrels, first roasted in hot ashes and then boiled with *ghanóhe:n(a)* (hominy made with ash lye) was, is, and doubtlessly always will be a favorite Cherokee dish. Its prepar-

---

[1] At about this period earth tremors in the old Cherokee country were of fairly frequent occurrence (see Mooney, *Myths of the Cherokee*, 471).

[2] Several hundred Cherokees, including Sequoyah and the future chief, John Ross, served with distinction in the Creek War under Andrew Jackson (see Grace Steele Woodward, *The Cherokees*, 131).

[3] Probably in reference to the seizure of a part of the Cherokee Nation by act of the Georgia legislature, December 19, 1829 (*ibid.*, 158).

[4] This is obscure. The literature makes no reference to any unusual event pertaining to Sequoyah in 1831.

[5] Could this refer to the 1835 appearance of Haley's Comet?

[6] The main body of the Cherokees was driven west in 1838–39.

[7] There was a payment to the Old Settler faction in September and October, 1851; the Ross faction was not paid until the following year (see Wardell, *A Political History*, 80–83).

[8] The War Between the States. MS in collection of authors.

ation was institutional at Keetoowah Society conclaves of the period of this document.

March 1, 1909

Now! I will write you a little, friend Digu:hl(e)di:sgi Wa:dh(i).

I am letting you know that on March 5th at Nv:ya Ghayv:-sadv́:i there will be soup to eat, and since I have asked you to work,[1] that is what you squirrel hunters will have to provide: bread, and a little meat, they[2] say; a little coffee, they say; a little money, they say, with which to buy a hog.

Now! Now I have just stopped writing.

Now! I greet you, friend Digu:hl(e)di:sgi Wa:dh(i).

I, Daye:wa Wahhya, just wrote this.[3]

CHRISTIAN MEDITATIONS (ca. 1910)

Occasionally one finds in some bundle of tattered literary odds and ends a scrap of paper preserving a passing mood of Christian reverie—a comment upon a Biblical passage, perhaps, or a speculation upon human destiny, or a prayer. Two specimens of such we present here.

The author of the first example was a resident of northern Adair County. He was a leader in the Redbird Smith nativistic movement in the first decade of this century. He was murdered by a white man about 1925.

The authorship of the second example, a meditation written upon a slip of coarse brown wrapping paper, is unknown. The document was found among the effects of a distinguished eastern Cherokee County shaman, who died about 1948, but it is not in his handwriting.

1.

This morning we are very thankful that we have awakened to well-being. Our God is compassionate: He brought it to be thus. He thought: "Let them alone; let them live." That is the

[1] Cherokeeism for "to serve in some official capacity."
[2] The officials in charge of the meeting.
[3] MS in collection of authors.

reason why we must come before Him, why we must pray to Him, why we must speak of Him.

We are weak, and He has freed us from sin. He is ever with us; He is very merciful. Our God and our Father lives Above: let all of us friends trust in Him.

2.

"The One who is called Jesus Christ is the Son of God. He has been sent down to earth," God, the Ancient One, says.

It is because of the Servant that I live, and our bodies are clothed. He planned it that way, and He said that we are not to be unclean while we live. He planned it: this earth on which we live is His.[1]

Dying Testimony of Cherokee Christians (1910–15)

Ani:lage:yv Ugí:dahl(i) was one of the greatest Cherokee preachers within memory. The white folk, who could not understand his burning words, deeply respected him for the way he walked among them; the Cherokees, who could understand, revered him. It is pointless to say that since his passing in 1956 his equal does not appear to be moving among the souls of his people, for no one has a right to expect his equal.

All of his ministerial life there was a compelling force in Ani:lage:yv. We have a photograph of him, taken in the springtime of his witnessing, in which the eyes of his handsome face fix the viewer with flames. Out of the pulpit he was wrapped in a quiet dignity; when he took the Bible in hand, he was transformed before men.

Although during his long ministry he served several congregations, he was longest identified with Salem Baptist Church in the tangled hill country of southeastern Adair County, Oklahoma. Not far from this church, in the summer of 1963, there were discovered, moldering upon the earth floor of a smokehouse, several manuscript books in Ani:-lage:yv's beautiful, small, and neat Sequoyah calligraphy. These notebooks present a remarkably full picture of the life and thought of a Cherokee minister, for Ani:lage:yv's power

[1] MSS in collection of authors.

in the pulpit was complemented by a scholarly attention to the details of his calling.

In a small pocket ledger Ani:lage:yv had carefully recorded the last words of some of his parishioners. The touching petition of a dying girl written in it, "Now! Ani:lage:yv, start the singing!" is profoundly symbolic: the singing, kindled in the hills by Ani:lage:yv, continues to sound.

1.

A:li Usana:li died on November 30, 1910, at the age of 19. She was baptized into the Salem Church congregation on August 16, 1908.

Her dying words were: "Nv:tsi, pray, and let us all pray.

"Now I am going to my Father's Place. I have found a Beautiful Place to live, and I have found my little children, my brothers.

"You must love me and follow me."

2.

De:nili Tsi:sghwa died January 4, 1911.

His dying words were: "Now I am going to my Beautiful Place where the buildings are made of gold. I have found God's Place. I see where I am going.

"I am in a hurry to go. Beloved ones, I am going to leave you. I have found the beautiful golden buildings of God."

He was an older preacher. He was a district councilman.[1]

3.

Tsa:wayu:ga Ayo:hlani was born January 21, 1901. She was baptized into the Salem Church congregation in September, 1914. She died January 16, 1915.

Her dying words were these: "I worked all the time, and now I have found where the Brightness is. Through the Narrow Door I am going into the Bright Lights, where there is gladness.

[1] Tsi:sghwa means Bird. This may have been the Peter Bird who was councilman from Flint District, 1897-99 (Emmet Starr, *History of the Cherokee Indians and Their Legends and Folk Lore*, 282).

"My father here below, I am anxious to find peace! Let me find peace, father!

"Now I find a boy, my brother,[2] where the Bright Rays are. There into where I am going, the children are happy. There I will be happy, where the happy and kind ones are, Christ's Land, that beautiful Resting-place that one can find if one has lived kindly here below.

"I prayed and I sang enough the whole time. I did right. And they are standing there with Lights near that Door for just a little while. As soon as I go in, they will put out one Light.

"Now! Ani:lage:yv, start the singing! You and I have already found out that it is a very Beautiful Place. It is truly the way the preachers say it is. It is blooming very beautifully. The flowers are so beautiful!"

Then she spoke to the children[3] and told them that if one lives a good life here, one will find happiness There.

4.

Gwe:di De:wi died February 12, 1915, at the age of 17. She was baptized into the Salem Church congregation, May 21, 1911.

Her dying words were: "Now! Mother, I have found a girl that belongs to us.[4] Now she and I are going. You must now work hard and follow us.

"I feel sorry for you that I have to leave. I feel sorry that I am leaving the family.

"Tsa:ni said . . ."

"Which Tsa:ni?" I asked.

"My uncle Tsa:ni," she said. "I am going to tell him how beautiful the Place is where the children live," she said.

"Now! Make my bed well. The wagon in which I am going

---

[2] In the collection of the authors is a register, in the handwriting of Ani:lage:yv, of Salem Church. This manuscript shows that a Li:wi Ayo:hlani, doubtlessly the brother referred to here, was baptized on November 7, 1909, and was killed on May 4, 1914.

[3] Probably her younger brothers and sisters.

[4] A deceased member of the family.

to ride is coming now. U:hwadhi has also gotten ready to go where Sida:ni⁵ is.

"Now! Mother, I am going down this Road."

5.

Wo:yi A:muno:yv:gi died December 7, 1915.
At the end he spoke: "All of us will live there Above.
"Mother, I love you.
"All that I owed is paid. I don't owe anything at this time.
"Hurry, Father, and climb up! I am already resting on High!"

He lived to be 19 years old. He was baptized into the Honey Hill[6] congregation, March 22, 1915. He was made deacon,[7] October 10, 1915.[8]

ANI:LAGE:YV SUMMARIZES HIS YEAR IN THE VINEYARD OF THE LORD (1914–15)

In one of his small notebooks Ani:lage:yv reviewed his activities during a year's incumbency as pastor of Salem Church. While there are those who would maintain that there is a fuller record written Above, nevertheless, the great preacher was quite specific concerning how he discharged his stewardship.

In evaluating this record, one must take into account the fact that inasmuch as Salem Church at this period had a membership of only 130 individuals, all abjectly poor, Ani:lage:yv's salary was but $150 per annum. In order to make ends meet, he had to devote a large part of his time working his small rocky farm on top of a mountain from which one can overlook miles upon miles of waving treetops.

From October 1, 1914
This below is the way I worked during the year at Salem Church:

1. The number of times that I preached   143

---

[5] Possibly the child referred to in n. 4.

[6] An eastern Adair County church that Ani:lage:yv also served during his career.

[7] A deacon only nineteen years of age is all but unheard of in Cherokee churches.

[8] MS in collection of authors.

2. The number of those that I accepted for baptism 23
3. The number of those that I baptized 15
4. I accepted by letter 2
5. Those weakened Christians that I accepted for rededication 92
6. Those that came and took the first step 2
7. Preaching in homes 18
8. I preached in the Cemetery 12
9. I prayed with individuals 88

FAIRFIELD SUNDAY SCHOOL ADOPTS REGULATIONS
FOR THE SICK AND THE DEAD (1915)

The activities of the Poor-Aid Society of the North Carolina Cherokees, some of which have been detailed as "... the management of funerals for deceased townsmen, the rebuilding and furnishing of someone's house after fire, or the donation of material aid and labor to the aged, handicapped, or infirm,"[1] are paralleled in Oklahoma by those of the Sunday school of the Cherokee community. The church itself, as an organization, tends to remain aloof from these eleemosynary activities, although every communicant is almost certain to be a member of the Sunday school, too.

Since in a sense it is the continuation of the aboriginal township organization, there is a secular tincture to the typical Sunday school of a Western Cherokee community. Whether he be Christian or pagan, nearly every member of the community attends it and supports it, and it, in turn, supplies social services to him. Some of these services are spelled out in detail in this document from Fairfield Baptist Church (Dhla:nuwo:h(i), in Cherokee), which is located a very short distance northeast of Stilwell.

SUNDAY SCHOOL ORGANIZATION REGULATIONS TO USE
FOR THE SICK

Section 1. The committee decided that which is to be written

[1] Raymond D. Fogelson and Paul Kutsche, "Cherokee Economic Cooperatives: The Gadugi," Bureau of American Ethnology *Bulletin 180* (1961), 105.

in the Sunday School Regulations: If, there where he lives, someone is sick or in some other form of distress, or if he is in great need of something, they [the Sunday school members] must help him in whatever he needs.

The Chairman must bring it to attention.

Section 2. We also added to the Sunday School Regulations: If, there where he lives, someone dies, as soon as possible the bell [of the church] must be rung to announce that someone passed away, and a paper must be attached to the door [of the church] to inform the many who it was that died, and all must truly help there where he is to be kept [prepared for burial].

The Chairman must take charge of the burial, and all must truly help.

Section 3. If someone dies, in carrying him, and in going out of the church, they must sing, and all those in his family, according to that which is written in the Organization Regulations, in walking, will be walking in two files. Then when they arrive at the cemetery, they must sing, and they must sing until the burial is finished.[2]

The Chairman will have the power to arrange matters right if he thinks something else is better.

Section 4. The bell is to be rung if someone is sick or in some other form of distress; the bell is to be rung once for five minutes. But if someone is dead, it is to be rung twice: for three minutes, and then after a wait of one minute, again for three minutes.

Now these above Regulations may be revised or amended by vote of the many.

Approved by me, Tsi:sdu Aghv́:hli, Chairman of the Committee.

Tso:wa Dvno:hwe:la:ni, Secretary
Approved April 26, 1915[3]

[2] The burial services provided a pagan by the fellow members of his Sunday school are likely to differ but little from those provided a Christian.

[3] MS in collection of authors.

Letter from Redbird Smith (1917)

This letter survived by the narrowest of margins. It was recovered in the summer of 1962 from a rain-sodden trash heap in a gully in the Sequoyah County, Oklahoma, community of mixed Creeks and Cherokees called Eveningshade by the whites.

It is a document of commanding interest, for from its wording one can see that it is almost certainly a call to one of the clan heads to attend a meeting for the purpose of enacting the *E:lohi Ga:ghusdv:d(i)* ("The Foundation of Life"), the supreme Cherokee ritual, ". . . reserved for the gravest of national emergencies, the final resort when the survival of the Cherokee people is in question."[1] One must remember that on March 26, 1917, the United States, and therefore the Cherokee people, stood on the brink of war. The *E:lohi Ga:ghusdv:d(i)* is traditionally performed ". . . when hostilities directly involving the Cherokee people impend or exist. . . ."[2]

Not only has the *E:lohi Ga:ghusdv:d(i)* never been witnessed by outsiders, but its very existence was unsuspected until it was reported by these authors.

> Here in Illinois District, March 24, 1917
>
> Beloved A:dawi He:nilv:
>
> Now! I have asked you to come to Illinois District, March[3] 6, 1917. At that time all Warriors are to be informed; also you are to bring tobacco to make the Sacred Medicine.
>
> I, Dhotsu:hwa Sighwani:da,
> Chief of the Keetoowah Organization.[4]

An Apprentice Medicine Man Goes to War (1918)

The battle skill and valor of thousands of young Cherokees are written into the histories of the regiments in which they served during World War I, and it is somewhat strange that we

---

[1] Jack Frederick and Anna Gritts Kilpatrick, "'The Foundation of Life': The Cherokee National Ritual," *American Anthropologist*, Vol. 66, No. 6, Part I (1964), 1386.
[2] *Ibid.*
[3] Indubitably a mistake for April.
[4] MS in collection of authors.

have never come across any letters in Sequoyah syllabary which tell St. Mihiel and the Meuse-Argonne from the Cherokee point of view.

The following is a diary note, not a letter, made by a young soldier who had been studying to be a medicine man when he was caught up in the whirlwind of war. It was inscribed in a manuscript notebook of conjurations that the Cherokee doughboy carried with him into combat.

There is something arresting in the picture of this student medicine man in the shell-rocked trenches, thousands of miles and thousands of years from home, pondering over some passage such as "Now! Listen! Red Panther, you have just come to make a radiant shadow."

The neophyte shaman eventually died from the effects of the wound he so casually mentions here, but not before he had had a successful dual career as medicine man and Baptist minister.

I left Texas on June 9th [1918].
I arrived in England on July 1st.
I arrived in France on July 10th.
We first fought one night, August 22nd.
On September 11th I was shot.
On September 12th I came to the hospital.
On September 13th I got up.
On October 13th I arrived where the soldiers stay.
On October 30th I arrived at the second place where the soldiers stay.

On Monday night, November 4, 1918, I came to the fourth place.[1]

The war was over here at Ilo:gwi[2] at 10 o'clock on November 11th.

---

[1] We wonder why he put the fourth military base in sequence before the third. Perhaps the installations were so numbered.

[2] Cherokee designations for European cities are apt to sound decidedly unlike anything that could be recognized by the inhabitants thereof. Since this word is meaningless as Cherokee per se, it must be an unidentifiable attempt at French.

At the third place where the soldiers stay, I arrived on Monday, November 18th at 11 o'clock.[3]

Two Love Incantations (ca. 1919)

Nearly all the entries in a pocket notebook in our possession pertain to such mundane matters as accounts of the sales of railroad ties (the hewing of which, up until about the period of World War II, was for the Oklahoma Cherokees a source of small amounts of ready, if exceedingly hard-earned, cash), and collections of money by the Gha:hl(i)se:ts(i) Tso:dalv Fire of the Keetoowah Society. But also written there are these two beautiful love incantations, the sheen upon which survives even the trauma of translation.

1.

Now! I have taken your heart;
I just took your breath.
Your heart has just entered into me:
I have just taken your thought.
Change your heart, and put it into
    the very middle of my soul!

2.

For you I have the eyes of the Yellow Mockingbird, the eyes of
    the Wild Goose, the eyes of the Deer, the eyes of the Wolf.
I have just come to make you sleepless throughout the night.
Tonight, without sleep, in anguish, you will ever be thinking of
    me, desiring me alone.[1]

Record of Money Collected by A:mó:hi Fire of the Keetoowah Society (1919)

A portion of the funds collected by each Fire of the Keetoowah Society was sent to the central Illinois Fire and deposited in a general fund from which loans and expenditures for charitable purposes were drawn. This document would appear to be the record of transmittal of money to the central Fire by the A:mó:hi Fire.

[3] MS in collection of authors.   [1] MS in collection of authors.

A:mó:hi ("Salt-place"), called Saline District in English, lay directly north of Tahlequah District. Its name was derived from salines along Grand River, which formed its western boundary.

June 25, 1919

Our A:mó:hi District Fire *Gadhi:yo*.
This is the money they collected. This is the amount . . $24.20
        Ane:sgwade:gi, Treasurer
        Ga:lanv:da Da:gwadi:hi, Secretary[1]

NOTATION BY A CONJURER CONCERNING A FEMALE CLIENT (ca. 1920)

The following brief memorandum, found among the papers of a deceased Cherokee County conjurer, relates the circumstances in the case of a woman (her "white" name is written upon the document as stated) who is seeking professional assistance in recapturing the diffused affections of her lover.

He is of the Wolf Clan.[1]
His name is Ghani:ga.[2]
He was the friend of Wa:li:si, whose name [in English] is written down.
They were friends, and he is angry at her.
She wants the one who is angry at her to walk behind her.[3]
She wants to make him walk following behind her by overcoming him with water.[4]

---

[1] MS in collection of authors.

[1] One of the seven Cherokee clans.

[2] For most incantations to be completely efficacious, the conjurer must know, and supply at the appropriate place or places in them, the name and clan of the individual against whom he is "working."

[3] To desire her.

[4] Most Cherokee conjuring is done facing east at the brink of a flowing stream. If the lover's anger was natural, and not due to witchcraft, Wa:li:si's "helper" almost certainly first removed the animosity with a *digv:ghe:-hw(i)sdo:dhi:yi* ("to make them forget with") incantation, and then "remade" (i.e., infused with magical powers) for her some tobacco to be smoked upon, or in the direction of, her lover. MS in collection of authors.

Dᴇ:ᴡɪ A?ʜᴡ(ɪ)ɢᴀᴅᴏ:ɢᴀ Hᴀs ᴀ Tʀᴀɴsᴘᴏʀᴛᴀᴛɪᴏɴ Pʀᴏʙʟᴇᴍ
(1923)

The formidable difficulties of transportation in the hilly wilds of the Oklahoma Cherokee country of the 1920's can be sensed in this earnest letter, from which there arises a humorous overtone when we consider that the entire crowflight distance that the writer was attempting to cope with was only about thirty miles. To traverse this the writer probably took a whole day to travel by wagon to Gore,[1] across the Arkansas River which was ferried in those days. There he took a Missouri Pacific train, from which he had to transfer to an east-west spur (no longer in existence) of the St. Louis and San Francisco which went through Welling.[2] Even then, as we see, his troubles were not over: someone had to take him south across Sugar Mountain, with its fearful wagon road, to his destination at Barber.[3]

If the writer, doubtlessly planning to pay a Christmas visit to his sister, arrived at his destination within three days after he set out, he was lucky.

Porum,[4] *Okla.*
Dec 7th 1923

Dear freind [sic]:―――
  Mr. J―― C―――.
  Barber, Okla.
I just wrote you a few words this morning.
Now! Beloved Uncle Uwe:da:sadh(i), I want you, or if you will ask some of your boys, to bring the wagon to Welling. We will arrive there on the morning of December 23rd. When we arrive there, have the wagon[5] there. All of my family are going to my sister's.

---

[1] A town in Sequoyah County.

[2] We:liní:i, a settlement in Cherokee County.

[3] Gwagwó:hi, a settlement in Cherokee County, now on the east side of upper Tenkiller Lake.

[4] A town in Muskogee County.

[5] Roads being what they were in the Oklahoma hills in 1923, automobiles were only slightly more than experimental, from the Cherokee point of view.

Do you hear? Don't disappoint us. You must do it for me on December 23rd.
What does my aunt say about meeting us at *Welling, Okla. Dec 23rd*
Please do this for me may I repaid you some time any how
[*on verso*]
Come! Come! and meet me at *Welling, Okla.* of December 23rd
Bring your wagon and take us to my sister A——— B———
Now! You must do this for me.
 I, De:wi A?hw(i)gado:ga
  D——— S———.[6]

List of Repentants at the Quarterly Meeting at Echota Church (ca. 1925)

Public confession of private sins is a fundamental element in the Cherokee practice of Christianity. Any out-of-the-ordinary church event—such as a revival, a quarterly meeting, or the visit of a renowned preacher—is apt to break out in a rash of confessions treasured up for an occasion worthy of them. In addition to the weaknesses to which all flesh is heir—fighting, the excess consumption of spiritous liquors, fornication, and the like—one is treated in these recitals to Cherokee specialties, such as the maintenance of multiple households and dabbling in witchcraft.

Those who were overcome by sin and who at the Quarterly Meeting here at Echota rededicated themselves:
1. Utso:sdo:sa, a member of Lees Creek Church.[1]
2. A:dawi Su:li, a member of Lees Creek Church.
3. Gane:lv:sa, a member of Round Springs Church.[2]
4. Tsv:go:na Tsa:n(i)sini, a member of Echota Church.[3]
5. Sina:sda Dhlv:di:sd(i), a member of Echota Church.

---

[6] MS in collection of authors.
[1] A church near Akins, Sequoyah County.
[2] Near Eucha, Delaware County.
[3] Near Stilwell, Adair County.

6. Ne:li Ghane:ga, a member of Echota Church.
7. Si:midhi Tsi:sghwa, a member of New Baptist Church.[4]
8. Nuwo:hiyu Sv:na, a member of New Baptist Church.
9. Sdhi:wi Adho:lanv:sdi, a member of Sequoyah Church.[5]
10. Ghv?sa?ni, a member of Cedar Tree Church.[6]
11. Ne:ni Udi:sga?hli, a member of Fairfield Church.[7]
12. Ne:si Udi:sga?hli, a member of Fairfield Church.

They were all accepted.[8]

A GOSPEL SONG IN SYLLABLES (ca. 1925)

Cherokees, by and large, are extraordinarily endowed musically. Since earliest contact with Christianity they have cultivated part-singing, and although now it is somewhat on the decline, their choral singing is still capable of being enormously moving.

The Cherokees are faithful customers of the companies in Arkansas, Texas, and Tennessee that specialize in the publishing of shaped-note editions of rousing gospel songs, and the majority of Cherokees can read the music, however mysterious may be the English words. Whatever may be the musical value of these songs, they tend to be somewhat complex rhythmically, with many rollicking syncopations.

Since the Cherokees cannot always read or pronounce the English texts, they frequently employ solfeggio, but as modified by the phonemes of Cherokee. *Do*, *mi*, *so*, and *la*, for example, offer no problems, but since there is neither an *r* nor an *f* in the language, *le* is substituted for *re*, and *gwa* (and sometimes *gwv*) for *fa*. *Ti* is available, but for some reason it is replaced by *si*. Needless to say, the strongly nasalized vowels bear small resemblance to their European counterparts.

A favorite song can be passed along to a friend without the necessity of parting with the cherished songbook in which it

[4] Near Stilwell, Adair County.
[5] Near Sallisaw, Sequoyah County.
[6] Near Tahlequah, Cherokee County.
[7] Near Stilwell, Adair County.
[8] MS in collection of authors.

appears. Its syllables are written down in Sequoyah syllabary, as is the following example from eastern Cherokee County:

So do mi mi le mi do:[1] gwv / mi le do do la do so:
Mi mi do do le mi le: / mi mi do do mi le do:
So do mi: do / mi le do: / do le mi mi mi le do:
Mi mi le: so / do mi mi le mi do:
Mi le do do la do so: / mi mi do do mi le do:[2]

ECHOTA SUNDAY SCHOOL MAKES PLANS FOR THE
COMING YEAR (1926)

The plans proposed below stand in need of some clarifications. The first item refers to a scheme for acquiring lumber to repair the flooring of the porch[1] of the church. The next item has to do with selecting and obtaining (by donation, if possible) beef on the hoof for the annual September Sunday School Convention, workers for which, with specific duties indicated, are named in the two items following.

The fifth item records the "calling for" or a *ga:du:gi*. The definition of the *ga:du:gi* in North Carolina, ". . . a group of men who join together to form a company, with rules and officers, for continued economic and social reciprocity"[2] does not hold for the main body of the Cherokee people in Oklahoma, where the *ga:du:gi* is composed of unpaid workers called together for a specific task in the interests of a private charity or community welfare. We are not informed concerning why the *ga:du:gi* mentioned here was formed.

July 25, 1926

The Sunday School Committee met and planned what to do in preparation for the coming year:
1. They made plans for boards for the porch.
2. They chose searchers for a cow: Aha:ma, Wa:di. Those who go get the cow they will choose later.

[1] The symbol: probably stands here for a prolongation.
[2] MS in collection of authors.
[1] A form of the verb *-adhl-* ("to floor") is used here.
[2] Fogelson and Kutsche, "Cherokee Economic Cooperatives, Bureau of American Ethnology *Bulletin 180* (1961), 87.

3. The meat-fryers: They chose U:ne:sdala. He is to choose his helpers.
4. The water-carrier: Digu:gh(o)di:sgi. He is to choose his helper.
5. There will be a *ga:du:gi* two weeks from this Wednesday.

Dhlvdi:sd(a), Chairman[3]

A Backslider Changes His Church Affiliation (1928)

Since this note was found among the papers of a deceased power in Echota Church, it must have been sent to that organization by Mulberry Tree officialdom. One detects in this message the faint odor of the peace offering to remove any possible taint of proselyting from the altar of Mulberry Tree, not only the First but the only Cherokee Baptist church in Mulberry Hollow, a few miles west of Stilwell, in Adair County, Oklahoma.

The bottom part of the note had been torn off.

October 28, 1928

Here at Mulberry Tree First Baptist Church we met. Sa:mi Dloge:si preached. When he finished preaching, the Lord's Door was opened. One person, overcome by sin, Ada:lo?di:sgi Aniyv:la, came forward. He belonged to the Echota Children of Christ, and we made him a part of us. We accepted him, and he became a member.[1]

Echota Sunday School Decides to Have a Cake Sale (1929)

Even as ". . . any committee of three Cherokees is perfectly capable of producing four opinions,"[1] the chance meeting of any two friends is apt to result in the election of a chairman and a secretary. It is not difficult to understand why the Cherokee Nation has engendered ornaments to the bar and the bench.

---

[3] MS in collection of authors.
[1] MS in collection of authors.
[1] Jack F. and Anna Gritts Kilpatrick, *Plains Indian Motifs in Contemporary Cherokee Culture*, 136.

The high seriousness that pervaded the endeavors of the committee at work here speaks out from the record that the chronicler—who was careful to state that he was merely the acting secretary—left. We wonder if when the decisions of the committee came before the minute inspection of the whole Sunday school, the honor bestowed upon the wives of two of the committeemen did not give rise to imputations of nepotism.

September 29, 1929

Now! It has just become time for the Committee to go to work.

Here is written the Chairman of the Committee: Tsi:mi Wa:lel(a).

Here are written the names of the members of the Committee: Dagv:wo?si, Ne?sini, and Tsu:n(a)sdu:di.

This is what we decided on Wednesday night: In a week, was the decision, we are to have a bread sale. We are doing this in order to pay for what we owe.

We just chose the cake bakers, written here: Ghe:ladi Tsu:-n(a)sdu:di and Wali:ya Dagv:wo?si.

And now before we adjourned, we decided to take up a donation.

That is all that the Committee just decided.

Tsu:n(a)sdu:di, Acting Secretary.[2]

ELECTION OF SERGEANTS-AT-ARMS (ca. 1930)

The observance of the amenities is skillfully practiced in Cherokee intramural politics—as witness the tact manifested in electing to the second vacancy the candidate defeated in the contest for the first post. One may be sure that the face of the candidate defeated for the second position was saved by subsequent elevation to honor even if some office had to be created on the spot.

There is no indication on this return concerning what organization held the election. It was found in a collection of

[2] MS in collection of authors.

papers, dating from about 1930, chiefly dealing with activities at Sycamore Tree Church.¹

CANDIDATES FOR SERGEANTS-AT-ARMS (TWO-YEAR TERMS)
1. Tse:gh(i)sini nominated Ditsuda:sgi Wi:li
2. Daye:ni Udi:sadiye:dv nominated Do:yi Nuwo:dhvn(a)
   Ditsuda:sgi——19
   Do:yi Nuwo:dhvn(a)—11
1. Daye:ni Udi:sadiye:dv nominated Do:yi Nuwo:dhvn(a)
2. Susa:ni nominated Tsa:ts(i) A:hyv́i:ní
   Do:yi Nuwo:dhvn(a)—19 (he won)
   Tsa:ts(i) A:hyv́i:ní—10²

HYMN BOOK OF U:NE:SDALA (ca. 1930)

Since the early part of the last century the Cherokees have produced Christian hymns. But a relatively few of them have survived: through incorporation into the *Cherokee Hymn Book*, the first edition of which was printed at New Echota, Georgia, in 1829; through oral tradition; or in batches of tattered family papers.

A representative Cherokee hymnodist was U:ne:sdala. His whole fame and most of his life were contained within a few square miles in the vicinity of Echota Indian Baptist Church in the dogwood hills of western Adair County. His practical Christianity would be somewhat more difficult to circumscribe, for his personal affairs had a tendency to wither under his willingness to sit up with the sick, or to make a coffin, or to serve on a committee of the church in whose adjacent graveyard he has slept now for about a decade and a half.

We remember him as a short and powerful man with strangely slumberous eyes, with little to say and much to sing. He had an opulent bass voice that could be counted upon in any vocal get-together. He read music fluently, although he knew little English.

U:ne:sdala must have written hundreds of hymns. He had

¹ See "Fragment of a Minute Book Recording a Revival at Sycamore Tree Church (1936)."
² MS in collection of authors.

a habit of penciling in a Cherokee text of his own underneath the words in a book of gospel hymns. Many of these books so emended are still borrowed and bartered about in his community.

Sometimes he would scribble a few hymns in a tiny notebook. We reproduce here, in a translation that is forced to sacrifice meter and rhyme, the contents of such a one of these.

I

It will not be long before we will be there
 in the Land of the Blessed where our Father is;
And when we get there in the Land of the Blessed,
 sin will have passed us by.

II

We will be working (even now, I suppose)
 there where the land ends.
Let us go, holding hands together (even now, I suppose)
 where we are going to rest.
We will have passed by that Place of Fear;
We will be helped (even now, I suppose).
One can see the house by the flowing water
 where we are going to rest.

III

Where the water rises it is beautiful;
 beautifully it sparkles.
Underneath, where it is cool
 we are going to rest.

IV

Now, I suppose, there is no darkness and no strife,
 there where we will live.
Now, I suppose, while there is still light,
 we tire.

V

We workers have been called now today
 from Jehovah's place on high.

Be not late: the Chief calls you;
the Chief calls you to work in His field.

VI

Now at this time one has to go on the road:
There is nothing here on earth but ever-present evil.
Now I will put down the heavy load I bear.
There it is good where the sun sets;
Here where I travel it is hot and cold.
In the place where I shall appear there is happiness;
One can be happy there in that blessed place.
It can never change: it is similar to the sunset.

VII

Now that it is his, he can be happy.
There is no sorrow and no sickness there.
There is no anxiety there. It is green.
It is beautiful there where it is green: for it blooms.
His beautiful songs are sounding there where it is green.[1]

"Going to the Water" Prayer for Longevity (1930)

It is not enough to say that the great body of medico-religious writings of the Cherokees is their true literature, and that it is also the only literature worthy of the name that was ever produced by a native North American society; it is more than that: it is one of the most profound and sublime productions of the creative spirit of man.

The "Going to the Water" prayers that have in manuscript survived in great numbers are of especial elevation and beauty. They relate to what Mooney and Olbrechts define as ". . . the most impressive of all of the ceremonies of the Cherokee and is performed only on important occasions, such as the birth of a child, the death of a relative or a very close friend, to obtain long life, in preparing for the ball game or for the green corn dance, at each new moon, to counteract the evil conjurations

[1] MS in collection of authors.

of an enemy, and in connection with some of the more important love formulas."[1]

Most of the "Going to the Water" rites are enacted at dawn while facing the sacred direction East at the brink of a flowing stream. In conjunction with a prayer appropriate to the purpose for which the ritual is performed, said either by a medicine man or, in some cases, by the participating layman, there is a symbolic bathing of the face and hands, or perhaps immersion.

This example of an Oklahoma "Going to the Water" prayer is perhaps a trifle shorter than the average specimen. Some are of great length. It was extracted from a notebook that had belonged to a shaman of the Tsegí:i community of south-central Adair County.

Now! Listen! Long Man,[2] very quickly You have just come to hear, You who took Your origin from the water-seep: very quickly You and I have just become one.

The White Pathway[3] lies in front of me: it is not crossed by the Blue.[4]

The white hair[5] from the crown of my head is to alight upon the White Chair,[6] which will be elevating me unto the sky.

Long Man, You who took Your origin from the water-seep, You have just come to put the White Walkingstick[7] into my hand.

(To "go to the water" if one wants to live until the children are grown.)[8]

---

[1] Mooney and Olbrechts, *The Swimmer Manuscript*, 233.

[2] The personification of running water.

[3] In Cherokee symbolism, white is the color of serenity and joy. The meaning here is: "The course of my life will be peaceful and happy."

[4] Blue is the color of misfortune and evil. See n. 3 above in "Charm for Assistance in War (1894)."

[5] The symbol of age.

[6] The symbol of repose and status.

[7] The symbol of a joyous and revered old age.

[8] MS in collection of authors.

A Temperance Song (ca. 1935)

The Cherokee Temperance Society was organized at New Echota in 1829, and after the Removal its constitution was published, in 1843. At various times temperance songs have been printed, some in the *Cherokee Hymn Book* itself.

As an organization, the Cherokee Temperance Society is seemingly defunct, though not from having won all Cherokees to a distaste for alcoholic beverages; the temperance sentiment still flourishes in the Christian churches, and there temperance songs are still sung. A typical example of one of these songs is this one, sung to music of unknown derivation. It is said to have been written by U:ne:sdala, of Echota, among whose effects a manuscript copy of it was found.

1. *You whisky-makers, think of the young people!*
Their parents cry over them; they weep for them.
Chorus: *How sad it is, if one has a taste for whisky,*
For it takes many from the earth!
2. *You whisky-makers, think of the children!*
Their parents cry over them; they weep for them.[1]

Prescription for Cardiac Disease (1936)

The Cherokees' interest in, and empirical knowledge of, botany must surely be second to that of no other native people of the Americas. Even the average layman's familiarity with plants and their respective medicinal properties is impressive; that of the medicine man can be awesome.

All Cherokee treatments do not require conjurations. Some merely necessitate the administration, without ceremony, of botanicals, although infusions and brews are prepared and taken with proper respect to certain traditional concepts, such as the removing of bark only from the east side of a tree, and the numerology of the dosage.

There exists a large corpus of prescriptions for such treatments. Occasionally one will encounter one of these remedies scribbled in a tattered notebook, or upon a scrap of paper folded into a book.

[1] MS in collection of authors.

Social Documents of the Cherokees, 1862-1964

We cannot say with certainty where this example originated. It was obtained in the Hungry Mountain community, at the eastern border of Cherokee County, Oklahoma. There is a date upon its verso.

> Wild rose[1]
> New Jersey tea[2]
> Indian cherry[3]
> Wild cherry[4]
> (For the heart)[5]

Fragment of a Minute Book Recording a Revival at Sycamore Tree Church (1936)

The ensuing notes were written upon two leaves, in a poor state of preservation, torn from a notebook that was approximately three and five-sixteenths inches by six and one-half inches in size. Their author—medicine man, minister, and secretary of the Sycamore Tree Cherokee Baptist Church—was a native of Delaware County who had married into the Sycamore Tree community. He died in 1938 at the age of about forty-five from the aftereffects of a severe abdominal wound incurred while serving in France with the 358th Infantry in World War I.[1]

"The Lord's Door" mentioned below is the traditional invitational hymn of Cherokee churches. No. 38 in the *Cherokee Hymn Book*, its initial phrase, "*Ehe:na tsadado:li:sdi tsa:sganv:tsv́:hi ú:yo*," would suggest that it is a translation of the hymn "Come, Humble Sinner," by Isaac Watts (1674-1748),

---

[1] *Rosa carolina*. The Cherokee name is *tsi:sduní:gisd(i)*. The roots are probably used in this remedy.

[2] *Ceanothus herbaceus*. The Cherokee name is *elí:sgal(a)*. The roots are probably used in this remedy.

[3] *Rhamnus caroliniana*. The Cherokee name is *ada dalo:níge*. The twigs are probably used in this remedy.

[4] Some species of *Prunus*. The Cherokee name is *gidha:hya*. Chips of the bark are probably used in this remedy.

[5] Although the specific malfunction of the heart for which these botanicals are prepared (doubtlessly by brewing) is not stated, it is probably tachycardia. MS in collection of authors.

[1] See "An Apprentice Medicine Man Goes to War (1918)."

but it is not. Its authorship, like that of the modal, "white spiritual" flavored tune to which it is sung, is unknown.

Sycamore Tree Church is situated about three miles south of the Cherokee County store called Barber, on the east side and toward the upper end of the loveliest body of water in Oklahoma, Tenkiller Lake.

We call attention to the collection of seven cents for the purpose of furthering the Word of God—a touching commentary upon the economic plight of the Sycamore Tree membership in the Great Depression year of 1936.

... and I spoke upon Chapter 15, Verse 24, written by Luke, and then we sang "The Lord's Door." Two, E:gi Ade:lagh(a)dhí:ya and Sa:dayi A:n(a)gwalu:v:sgi, came for baptism, and at 2:30 on Sunday, October 25, 1936, I baptized her [sic]; and at 7:30 in the evening Siga:wi and I preached the Gospel. We did not base it upon the 1st and 5th; and also we sang "The Lord's Door." No one came forward. We dismissed.

On Sunday, October 25, 1936, I collected money, $.07, for the purpose of continuing the Word, and in the evening we preached the Gospel. We based it upon John 1:9, and we sang "The Lord's Door." No one came forward. We dismissed.

Sycamore Tree Church, October 28, 1936. The third evening we had a separate prayer meeting. When we had finished our meeting, I preached the Gospel based upon Matthew 23:32, 42, and 43,[2] and we sang "The Lord's Door." One, I:sili, came forward, and we accepted him, and then we dismissed.

October 31, 1936. We had church at Sycamore Tree, and I preached the Gospel based upon John 5, the 28th and 29th verses. I talked, and we sang "The Lord's Door." One, Tsughilv:di, came forward, and we accepted him.

November 1, 1936. When the Sunday school meeting was over, I preached the Gospel based upon Acts 17:2, 3 and Mat-

---

[2] Actually the twenty-third chapter of St. Matthew has only thirty-nine verses.

thew 8, the 34th verse; and then we sang "The Lord's Door" and one, Seli:si, came forward. We accepted her. We dismissed.[3]

Sycamore Tree Church Agrees to Supply Workers for a Convention at Echota Church (1938)

The September convention of the several Cherokee Baptist churches has long been an important tribal event (most Cherokee Christians are Southern Baptists), but whereas formerly a specific church was selected to be host, there is now a central meeting place at Cedar Tree, a few miles east of Tahlequah.

The document below is an official communication from Sycamore Tree Church (Cherokee County) to Echota Church (Adair County), host of the forthcoming convention. One notes that arrangements are being made approximately one month ahead of time.

August 21, 1938. Here at Sycamore Tree.
What you members of both of the Church and Sunday school at Echota were depending upon me to do, I, E:tsini Ghani:gwayo:gi, have accepted. I am bringing enough bakers, 8 in number, and here are their names written:
1. Tsiyo:se Tso:wa
2. La:yili Tsu:n(a)sdu:di
3. Go:dhane Sali:gu:wa
4. A:li Di:sdo:sgi
5. E:gi Gha?lada
6. Li:si Suge:da
7. Tsinv:na Tsu:n(a)sdu:di
8. Sa:li Ade:lagh(a)dhí:ya
9. Gadu:yui Tsu:n(a)sdu:di

These are all the workers they chose. This the number—18 in all.

The names of the women who are to be the cooks' helpers are written, and the men workers also. They thought it was good to

---
[3] MS in collection of authors.

go, and they agreed to help all of you in whatever you ask. Here are their [the men's] names written:
1. Unv:dagwv Sali:gu:wa
2. Uwe:dhiyu:la Digo:ye:sgi
3. Su:ye:dv Tsu:tsayo:sdi
4. Adawo:sgi Tsu:n(a)sdu:di
5. Tso:wa Tsu:n(a)sdu:di
6. Di:ga?lisgi Sgaye:tsa
7. Sighwani:da Dihl(i)dhade:gi
8. Tsa:yi Tsi:mi
9. Li:wi A?dhohi:sgi

Secretary of both Church and Sunday school,

Tso:wa[1]

A Bundle of Love Letters (1938–39)

It is as difficult to reconstruct a flower from a few petals as to hypothesize a romance from a few letters, such as these, that have survived it. These missives attest, however, to the idyl enacted against the green wilderness of Cherokee County having possessed certain elements cherishable by playwrights: the gentleman was elderly, the lady ardent; the gentleman was cautious, the lady given to a love of adornment.

Since these letters are from the hand of the lady, we have observed the propriety of concealing the identity of everyone mentioned by name. We have also made minor repairs upon the grammar of the writer in such places as where an excess of affection led her into error.

I

Beloved, don't hate me. Beloved, I think you ought to send me a letter for me to read. If you think that you are going to give me those dresses, I will be looking for them next week. When you send them to me, you must write me a letter telling me what you think.

Don't forget that I live. It is plain that until I die, I am your

---

[1] MS in collection of authors.

A———. B———, I want us to live together by ourselves, for us to think for ourselves.

II

May 9, 1938

B———, how are you getting along? Don't you know I have been looking for the clothes? Quickly send me a letter telling me what you are thinking. You must let me know if you are going to give them to me or not. If you are going to give them to me, be quick. I am in a hurry.

They say that you have C———. I suppose it is true, for I must be too old now. I think that you dislike me. Now you and your loved one will live together. I have been waiting a long time for us to get married, for you had said that we would.

My brother D——— and I are going next week. He wants to see you, and I do, too. I want to find out something.

It is time to send me clothes, and if you send them, I won't bother you for a long time, but if you don't send them, you will see something bad. I truly love you, and I continue to love you.

Now! I suppose that when you send me a letter, you will tell me what you are thinking—if you are prepared to give me clothes.

Now! I greet you, dear B———.

I, A———, ugly A———.

I will be looking for a letter—and clothes.

III

December 5, 1938

Some of my family don't want to see you. Don't come here. Let's see each other in Tahlequah, on the 17th of this month, a week from Saturday. I'll be there. You must come there if you want us to talk.

Don't have C———with you. I am certainly afraid of your friends nowdays, and your evil children. You're not a man. You're lazy. I guess C——— got all the rings you were telling about, and they are hers. Your children curse me.

E——— F——— and I have not forgotten. I don't want to see

you, but if you want to talk with me, you must come to Tahlequah. We will tell you something.

I came a long time ago, and in the morning I am going with G——— H———. Here I am with my sister as long as she is alive. I don't stay at home. I live away off. More and more I will not be at home. Saturday they will come for me.

I, A——— G———, wrote this.

IV

You must send my shoes, size 6–½, and silk hose by Saturday. I will be looking for them. I love you, B———.

Your A———.

V

January 30, 1939

My only beloved B———, I'm glad that I saw you, and you must send me my shoes, size 6, and also hose. I will be looking for them Monday.[1]

Diagnoses of a Medicine Man (ca. 1940)

Found among the soiled and crumpled papers of an eastern Cherokee County shaman who died (from the witchcraft of an enemy, rumor has it) in the spring of 1962 was a sheet upon which he had scratched down some notes concerning the cases of a couple of clients.

The first case was obviously that of a young man whose affairs of the heart were not prospering, and who had come to the medicine man for advice and help. The latter made a note to the effect that he had "inquired" into the situation (performed a divining ceremony) and had learned that through the witchcraft of an enemy the young man had been rendered supernaturally repugnant to women. Evidently the medicine man did not consider the case to be a very serious one, and rather routinely ascribed to it a hopeful prognosis if proper measures were taken. We suspect that at least one of those proper measures was the teaching to the young man of a procedure called *ado:dhlvhi:soʔdhí:yi* ("to remake oneself"), a

[1] MSS in collection of authors.

ritual for the purpose of making one irresistible to the opposite sex.

The second case was a serious matter. The woman was being conjured by "thinkers," i.e., persons who harbored ill-will against her and were creating her illness. Her death was inevitable unless countermeasures were taken. The medicine man's observation about what must be done in her case is not well stated, but what he meant was that she would have to come to him so that he could "take her to the water" (go at dawn to the brink of a stream) and enact a ceremony for the purpose of breaking the power of the "thinkers."

1.

I inquired[1] about Tso:sgayoyí:yi Isa:yi, and this is what I found out, this is the way it is: he has surely been blocked, and women have been made to avoid him, but he can overcome if he is helped.

2.

Dayi:ni Dla:ne:na is sick over there where she is. It is true that persons have "thought" her sickness, but she can be helped. But one has to "work"[2] quite a bit. I cannot help her where she is unless we use that "medicine"[3] for the "thinking" of persons. Then she would be all right.[4]

PRAYER FOR DIVINING WITH LEAD (ca. 1940)

As previously stated, the Cherokees divine by various methods: by a plummet, coin, or stone suspended upon a string; by means of floating beads or needles; through the observation of ceremonially roiled water, etc. This extract from a notebook from south-central Adair County, Oklahoma, is an example of the prayer said before observing the motions of a suspended

[1] Cherokee divining is done in a number of different ways. The method that was probably used here was that generally preferred one for ascertaining the cause of sickness: the medicine man stirs running water with a stick and then studies its appearance.
[2] Euphemism for conjuring.
[3] Euphemism for a conjuring ritual.
[4] MS in collection of authors.

plummet. The point of the compass toward which the piece of lead moves supplies the answer sought, East being the "affirmative" or "favorable" direction.

Apportioner,[1] in Your resting place in the Seven Heavens,[2] quickly I have just come to let You know.
From Your resting place Above, very quickly You have just come to let me hear.
(To learn something. Lead is used. Four times.[3])[4]

Comment Upon World War II (1940)

The Bible in its entirety has never been translated into Cherokee—only the New Testament and portions of the Old Testament. Various books, as soon as they were translated, were issued separately, but upon several occasions books and portions of books were issued bound together. A mutilated copy of one of these compilations, seemingly not mentioned in Hargrett[1] but apparently dating from the 1850's, came to light in Tahlequah in 1962. Its blank pages contain several generations of scribbling, in Cherokee and in English, in faded ink and in pencil: demographic data, columns of figures, fugitive notes, and the like. Upon the blank verso of the title page of the Gospel of John (1854 edition) is someone's apocalyptic comment, in Cherokee, upon World War II:

March, 1940
Across the ocean in Germany they are at war. In the smoke of the fire one sees the rain of blood.[2]

Letter from the Chief of the Keetoowah Society (1941)

This letter from the chief of the Keetoowah Society to the wife of an official in his organization contains the predictable:

[1] See n. 4 to "Address Upon the Keetoowah Society (1901)."
[2] Cherokee theology conceives of seven tiers of celestial regions.
[3] Being concerned with a relatively minor matter, this prayer requires but four iterations. More important issues necessitate seven.
[4] MS in collection of authors.
[1] Hargrett, *Oklahoma Imprints*.
[2] MS in collection of authors.

a report on family health (writer and recipient were doubtlessly relatives), and a tidbit of Keetoowah news.

Yo:nv́wi:n(v) was the son and successor of Chief Redbird Smith, and one observes that, Cherokee fashion, the first name of his father is written as the surname of the son.

November 15, 1941
Here in Illinois District[1]

Sa:lada Tsa:ts(i):

This morning I just wrote you a little bit.

You were asking about us nearby, how we are getting along. Tsiwo:n(v) and E:ni Igo:di[2] are not well, but the rest of us are well. We seem to be all right every day.

Tsa:ts(i) Wi:li[3] is surely at home over there now. He was here a week ago. They have taken away the *gadhi:yo*, and it is at Marble City,[4] he said. Now that they have taken the *gadhi:yo* there, they have set a time for a meeting.

Now! That is all that I just wrote.

I,Yo:nv́wi:n(v) Dhotsu:hwa[5]

Two Children's Remedies (1942)

It would appear that formerly the average Cherokee household possessed a manuscript collection of conjurations for minor domestic emergencies: cuts, burns, nosebleeds, and the like. A little notebook from the Echota community, containing two conjurations applicable to commonly-met-with children's ills, is translated here. Its probable date is established by a calendar printed upon the back cover.

1.

(This written below is to doctor with when their navels protrude. One warms it for them; one uses coals.)

---

[1] Illinois District in the sense of Keetoowah Society jurisdiction.
[2] These are feminine names, those of individuals probably related to both writer and recipient.
[3] The husband of the recipient.
[4] A village, known to the Cherokees as Ga:dayó:sd(i), in Sequoyah County.
[5] MS in collection of authors.

My Apportioner!
You will heal for me Your grandchild.
Yellow!¹ Yellow! Yellow! Yellow!
"Relief!" I will be saying.

2.

(This written below is to doctor with when they are ill with the "black."² Soaked black.³ Top of the head, hands, feet, chest.⁴)

Ha! It was the Rainbow that covered you with a rainbow.⁵
Ha! You⁶ decided that one was not to be tracked.
Ha! Right here Above rests the Apportioner.
You Apportioner! He has tracked you.⁷
You Apportioner! Uncover it!⁸
You Apportioner! Uncover it!
You Apportioner! Uncover it!
You Apportioner! Uncover it!
You Apportioner! Put it in it!⁹
You Apportioner! Put it in it!

[1] There are several species and subspecies of the "yellow." The type to which the treatment written here is applicable is known as "navel yellow." One of its diagnostic symptoms is soreness and distention of the abdomen in the region of the navel. This conjuration is said as the medicine man warms his hands over coals. He then presses firmly upon the area affected. This procedure is done four times.

[2] The "black," from the white man's point of view usually a circulatory disorder, is a sub-type of the yellow. It is characterized by dark circles under the eyes, vertigo, etc.

[3] The botanical employed is the root of wild senna (*Cassia marilandica*). It is soaked in cool "new water" (freshly drawn running water).

[4] The part of the body specified here is "blown" with a small amount of the liquid off the soaked wild senna root after the conjuration is said.

[5] Seeing "lights," "rainbows," and "spots" frequently attends the vertigo of the "black."

[6] "You [the Rainbow] decided to hide so that you could not be found" is the meaning here.

[7] "The Apportioner [God] has found you [the Rainbow]."

[8] The Rainbow.

[9] "Imprison the Rainbow in some sort of container" is the meaning of this sentence.

You Apportioner! Put it in it!
You Apportioner! Put it in it!
"Relief!" I will be saying.[10]

LU:SI REPORTS ON THE ILLNESS OF U:SGOGI:D(A) (1942)

Letters of the genre of this one must have been written by the thousands during the period in which the Sequoyah syllabary was in general use. The smallness of the number of those that have apparently survived is something at which to wonder.

Since the addressee was a Keetoowah Society official, seemingly we have here a progress report by a female relative, perhaps a daughter, of another official for whom illness is making problematical attendance at some meeting.

Webbers Falls,[1] *Okla.*
May 5, 1942

A:dawi:

We[2] are writing you this letter. You told us to write you a letter.[3]

U:sgogi:d(a) appears to be all right. He was not so restless last night.

"I plan to come, if I can," he said.

That is all that I just wrote.

I, Lu:si O:gan(a)sdo:da[4]

LETTERS FROM A PATIENT IN CLAREMORE INDIAN HOSPITAL (1943)

Four letters, found in a huge old trunk near Candy Mink Spring, limn the outlines of an amusing little drama: A man, probably a young man, is treated for an eye disorder at the Claremore Indian Hospital; when he is discharged, he is unable to go home because he cannot come by the $2.50 still lacking

---

[10] MS in collection of authors.
[1] A town on the Arkansas River, in Muskogee County.
[2] The person who is ill and the actual writer?
[3] A:dawi must have requested a report on the illness of U:sgogi:d(a).
[4] MS in collection of authors.

for bus fare. If this be a study of poverty, it is also a study of patience.

Three of these artless letters are to a woman, the writer's mother, no doubt; one of them, No. 2, is to a male friend or relative. All contain that standard feature of Cherokee letter writing, solicitude for the health of relatives, friends, and neighbors, and joyful volleys of greetings to them.

1.

May 12, 1943

This evening I just wrote you, Sida:ni Ne:di. This is all—they have delayed my discharge. Just this morning they treated my eye. But I do not think anything of it;[1] I am happy about it. I just thought I would tell you this: my body is all right.[2]

Now about you—I hope all of you are getting along well. To all of our neighbors I am sending my greetings, and Tsu:wi He:nil(i) I also greet.

Now! That is all that I, Ghanvtsu:hwa Ne:di, just wrote.

All of you must send me a letter soon. Tell me if the boy is getting along all right, and Susa:ni, both of them, and my aunt.

2.

May 28, 1943

This afternoon I just wrote you, Li:wi Aha:ma. I received a letter from you. It is all right to be here. Up here there are many soldiers.[3] Up here this is the way it is—airplanes are always flying, and there are many floods.

It surely is not lonely. There are many women here. The little woman will still live.[4] But I suppose the girls won't be crying from loneliness. Next week I will leave.

I greet all the family and your neighbors.

Now! That is all I just wrote.

I, Ghanvtsu:hwa Ne:di

---

[1] I.e., "I do not mind the pain."

[2] Probably the verdict after a general physical examination.

[3] One remembers that this letter was written during World War II.

[4] His wife or girl friend at home? The meaning appears to be that she will not die from jealousy.

3.

May 28, 1943

This afternoon I am writing you, Sida:ni Ne:di. I received the letter you wrote. I was very happy to hear that you are getting along well. I am well at this time.

Now I can leave anytime, as soon as I get enough money—$2.00. I asked for $4.00 before, and I received it, and then the second time I asked for $2.50. That is all that I will be wanting. When I get it, I can leave. The doctor has already discharged me, but I will still get my eyes doctored until I leave.

I send my greetings to Tso:wa. Don't let him worry about anything. To all I say "Hello!"—and also to Tsiga:dhuhwi:sdi I send my greetings, and to Tsu:wi.

Now! That is all that I, Ghanvtsu:hwa Ne:di, just wrote.

Ne:li and family came.[5] To all those written here: we will see each other soon.

4.

Here in the Oklahoma Hospital, June 3, 1943

This morning I just wrote you a few words, Sida:ni Ne:di. I am letting you know that I have been discharged. I was discharged three weeks ago. I almost left last night, but I was short of money. If I had had enough money, I would have come home. But it wasn't enough. I had asked for $2.50 before, and that is what I look for daily. But I believe that the money will arrive any time.

I hope Tso:wa is well, and also Tsu:n(a)ghilv́:di, and also Susa:ni. I think about you all the time. Tsa:ni O:hla and I both are in here.

Now! That is all that I, Ghanvtsu:hwa Ne:di, just wrote.

Now! I say "Hello!" to all of you, and also to all of your neighbors.[6]

FRAGMENT OF A MYTH (1944)

This myth, left unfinished by the writer, is unknown to us.

[5] Relatives or friends from home must have visited him.
[6] MSS in collection of authors.

We have not encountered it in the literature, printed nor manuscript, nor have we found it as oral tradition. Something about the formation of the Sequoyah symbols suggests that the writer was a woman perhaps advanced in years; but concerning the identity of the writer we have no clue, nor do we have any idea why literary inspiration failed at a juncture so critical to the story line and our curiosity.

Now! Tonight I will write a few words, September 25, 1944. There lived three boys who were brothers.

One decided: "I am going to travel to the West," and he said, "A year from now you two must return here. Then you will find out what happened to me. It will be evident to you: when you two wash your faces, your noses will bleed,[1] and by this you will find out that something happened to me," they were told.

And when they arrived at where their grandmother lived: "Now! Make me some *ghv:hwisi:da*,"[2] he [the brother who had decided to travel] told his grandmother. "I am going to travel toward the West," he told her.

Sure enough, his best attire was made ready for him. Then he left.

In his traveling, sometime later, he met an old man.

"How fortunate! You may have some food with you. I am truly becoming famished," he told the boy.

"Yes, I certainly have food with me," he [the boy] told him, "but it is all for my own use," he stated.

"All right," he was told.

"I am going toward the West," said the boy ...[3]

Uwe:da:sadh(1) Writes of Fence Posts and Thieves (1945)

The Cherokee allotments in Oklahoma were for the most part originally covered with stands of valuable timber—walnut,

---

[1] This motif has not been previously reported in Cherokee myths.
[2] Parched corn meal. Because of its nutritive qualities combined with its portability, it formerly was the principal sustenance prepared for a journey.
[3] MS in collection of authors.

Social Documents of the Cherokees, 1862–1964

hickory, oak, and ash. Since the boundaries of these holdings generally were, and still are, poorly defined, often in dispute, and frequently merely disregarded, tracts of rough and wild woodland, unfenced and unprotected, have ever provided temptation to white loggers.

The ensuing letter, from a resident of the Sugar Mountain community in eastern Cherokee County to someone unidentified, diplomatically suggests that the recipient might as well sell the writer some fence posts since white thieves will otherwise in all likelihood be the ultimate beneficiaries.

March 8, 1945

Did you get this money that I sent? If you got it, let me know. If you got the check that I sent you, I want to hear. I sent it to you this past February.

I am asking you for fence posts to be given to me. I am asking you for them when you decide that you want to see a little money.[1] You know that there are truly very wicked white thieves stealing from your land. Nowadays they would kill, if necessary.

Now! That is all that I, Uwe:da:sadh(i) Sa:wali, just wrote. If you are giving them[2] to me, write me a letter.[3]

A Medicine Man's Dream (1946)

One of the most unusual Cherokee documents we can recall having seen is this letter which we think was written by an aged medicine man to his middle-aged son, also a medicine man—or perhaps at the time the letter was written, an apprentice medicine man. It is traditional among the Cherokees that a shaman must have gray hair before he enters into active practice.

While the Cherokees put much emphasis upon the import of dreams,[1] no interpretation of this one was attempted.

[1] The breezy idiom "to see money" equates with "to be paid."
[2] The "long" quality built into the verb reminds us that the writer is referring to fence posts.
[3] MS in collection of authors.
[1] See Mooney and Olbrechts, *The Swimmer Manuscript*, 35–37.

March 2, 1946

Now! This is the way I dreamed last night:

Tsi:mi Tsu:sghwali:sd(a) was very sick, I saw. He was suffering in his neck and in his chest. And then he asked me to doctor him.

"I cannot do anything for you unless I cut you."[2]

"All right, then," he said, "if that's the way it has to be," he said.

Sure enough, I did cut him, and then after I had cut him, I doctored him with the "they are shot" medicine.[3] And after I had doctored him, I put him to bed.

Immediately I:sda[4] also went to bed on the other side of him. I suppose that is who was making the sick one fall out of bed. Then I kept putting him back to bed again.

Now at this time I asked him: "Now! How is your neck?" I asked him.

"Very good indeed! Much better!" he told me.

"All right," I said to him.

I was very much afraid to do him that way, to cut him. I took out different things—for instance, chips[5] that were in him and that seemed to make him swollen. That is what he saw when I showed him.

"That is what defiles one," he said.

Now! That is all.[6]

---

[2] Cherokee surgery is rudimentary and entered into cautiously. The average medicine man is inclined to regard the surgery of the white doctor as a confession of failure.

[3] "They are shot" is a circumlocution for a foreign object, or foreign objects having been introduced by witchcraft into the body of a patient. The treatment is to incise the site affected and to suck out the intrusive material (the *ga:dhidv*) by means of a small section of deer horn, or else to apply a poultice. Appropriate conjurations accompany the procedure.

[4] Probably the wife of the patient.

[5] Bits of wood, strings, and insects are common forms of the *ga:dhidv*.

[6] MS in collection of authors.

Social Documents of the Cherokees, 1862–1964

Diary Comments upon the Moon and Money (1946)

In a small and thin red pocket notebook, provided to the public for the primary purpose of making known the unassailable superiority of a certain patented farm product, are scribbled down some diary notes that lend insight into some of the diarist's chief interests toward the end of his long life—the appearance of the night sky of Oklahoma, and the size and continuity of his old-age assistance.

To write upon this book: June 3, 1946. A large star hung near the moon this month. It was this way: ☽*.

June 9, 1946. The moon rose just at night-fall. The moon at first had a tail toward the west, this way: ◄☽.
Later, on the east side, the same thing happened for a little while.

June 12, 1946. In Stilwell Tsi:sdu and I agreed that old-age assistance was to be paid to me in full. I paid $1.25.

June 17, 1946. In Tahlequah I borrowed money for the purpose of helping Me:li get assistance. I paid $4.50 in all.

June 12, 1946. I went to visit Digano:tsali. I came home on the 17th.

My number: VR 21267. Me:li's number: VR 32365.

Me:li rented farming land. It was rented to Tsa:ni Wahhya.

She lent me money August 3, 1946. On March 23, 1945, I received a letter with $50.00 for renting six acres in cultivation. It was rented for a year.

August 7, 1946.

I gave Tsi:sdu	$10.00
What Me:li has lent me	6.00
In Stilwell I first paid Me:li	.75
And I paid	4.50
The second time I paid	5.00
	$26.25

The old-age check came, and I got it June 30, 1942.

July 1, 1942	$33.00
1943	36.00
1943	40.00
1944	21.00
1945	30.00
June 15, 1945, I was getting	30.00
September 1, 1946, I got in all	38.00[1]

LETTER ABOUT FISHING-POLE CANE AND HEALTH (1947)

Letter writing in the Sequoyah syllabary is on the brink of extinction. We have never seen any statistics relative to reading and writing Cherokee that would be applicable to the Oklahoma branch of the tribe, but it has been stated that less than 10 per cent of the Eastern Cherokees are now literate in the syllabary.[1] The percentage of Western Cherokees may be even smaller: very few individuals under the age of fifty can read their own language, even fewer can write it.

Nowadays friendly letters are written almost exclusively by oldsters. A sample of such is this note from a Delaware County shaman (he died about 1962) to someone unidentified.

January 14, 1947

Now! I will write a letter for you, Salo:li Si:gwitsi, to read. Now! Are you well? I am fairly well.[2]

Now! We are going over there. I am going to Ghwayó:hi[3] to hunt for cane to hang a fishing line on.[4]

[1] MS in collection of authors.

[1] Raymond D. Fogelson, "Change, Persistence, and Accommodation in Cherokee Medico-magical Beliefs," Bureau of American Ethnology *Bulletin 180* (1961), 218.

[2] Probably so as not to invite disease, seemingly no Cherokee will admit possessing perfect health.

[3] "Huckleberry-place." This is the name of the town of Pryor, in Mayes County. It should be spelled Gh(u)wayó:hi.

[4] Since Cherokees are seldom lukewarm about eating fish flesh—some being inordinately fond of it, others holding it in abhorrence—we wonder if fish were not aboriginally taboo to some segment, or segments, of Cherokee society.

Social Documents of the Cherokees, 1862–1964

Now! I am going over to your house. I am going to visit you overnight.

Now! You must write me a letter of your own writing.

Now! Da:gi Wahhya[5] is still sick—the reason, I suppose, is because she is old.

Now! That is all I just wrote. I send my greetings: "Hello!" all.[6]

A Cherokee Recalls to Mind the Alliance of 1730 (1948)

In a small yellow notebook advertising a brand of snuff is the hodgepodge of entries that one would expect to find: dates of births and deaths, expenditures, names and addresses; but squarely in the middle of those run-of-the-mill jottings for the year 1948 is to be found this dramatic backward leap of 218 years.

We surmise that the writer had extracted from some manuscript chronology this memorial of the visit to the British Court of seven Cherokee chiefs[1] and headmen, during which the alliance known as the Articles of Agreement was entered into (actually on September 30, 1730) between these leaders and the Lords Commissioners.[2]

They agreed at Gu:le-disgo:hnihi[3] on June 30, 1730. The English were heard for the second time[4] concerning the guiding of the Brown People[5] here in America.[6]

---

[5] Probably the wife of the writer, whose name was Wahhya.

[6] MS in collection of authors.

[1] In the literature the English spelling of the names of these Indians is so fantastic as to preclude any easy arrival at what they really were. The white man has ever exhibited a distinct gift for insensitivity to the phonemes of Indian languages.

[2] Woodward, *The Cherokees*, 64–67.

[3] "Dove-place" or "Pigeon place" probably an old name for London.

[4] The "first time" must have been the council at Nequassee on April 3, 1730, at which Sir Alexander Cumings induced the Cherokees to accept Moytoy as "Emperor" (Woodward, *The Cherokees*, 63).

[5] The Cherokees never refer to Indians as "red" men, or people; they are always designated as "brown."

[6] MS in collection of authors.

REGULATIONS FOR OBSERVANCE OF MEMORIAL DAY AT SYCAMORE TREE CEMETERY (1955)

One senses what has been designated the Cherokee "genius for institutionalization"[1] in the Chairman, referred to below, basing his apologia for present-day procedures in decorating graves upon a regulation of 1909. One also senses some of the sad realities of Cherokee life: the toll exacted by wars not of Cherokee making (the "new soldiers" were victims of the Korean conflict of 1950–53) and the rate of infant mortality.

Just as in 1909, brightly colored artificial flowers are still made by families of the dead; but other than flags and real flowers, artificial floral work constitutes practically the only decoration of Cherokee graves. The elaborate mortuary embellishments of such a culture group as the Latin Americans, for example, contrast strongly with the solemn and simple Cherokee concepts.

May 30, 1955

Chairman Uhyv:dhlo:yi Sdui:sdi opened the meeting at Sycamore Tree Cemetery Decoration:

" 'To begin, there will first be a song, and then a prayer, and then the flower-makers will place the flowers here in the Cemetery. May 30, 1909.'

"Now it is May 30, 1955. That is what we base this upon here today when we meet here in Sycamore Tree Cemetery.

"Now these are the Chairmen:
> Suda:ni Une:gada
> Uhyv:dhlo:yi Sdui:sdi
> Ganv:dho:hi Ga:dhlinuli:sgi."

May 30, 1955

Old soldiers laid away and memorialized—3 in number.
New soldiers—4 in number.
Children buried during the past year—4 in number.
Adults—1.

[1] Raymond D. Fogelson, review of Fred Gearing, *Priests and Warriors: Social Structures of Cherokee Politics in the 18th Century*, 728.

First the ground will be cleared in order to place the flowers.
1. La:wan(i) Nuwo:dhvn(a)—preacher for the old soldiers.
2. I:nagi Ghu:wv—will afterward talk in English.
3. Sali:gug(i) Ghodé:sgi.

All of the preachers will offer a dismissal prayer.[2]

The Pastor of Echota Church Writes to one of His Deacons (1957)

Primarily as a result of the critical shortage of qualified ministers, Christianity is seemingly on the decline among the Oklahoma Cherokees today. It is quite common for a minister to have to serve several churches simultaneously, and he may live at the distance of a county or two away from them.

Very characteristically, the minister wrote this post card from Tahlequah, in Cherokee County, to one of his deacons in Adair County.

Oct. 8, 1957

Brother J——— N———:
I cannot come to my church. I am not well. I think I have the *"Flu."* On *Sat. Oct.* 12th, I will be there if I am well. I feel sad because I cannot come as a result of what has happened.[1] We will see each other *Sat.* if God thinks it is all right.

from P——— R———[2]

Minutes of Echota Sunday School (1959)

The meticulosity with which Cherokees ordinarily keep church and Sunday school records is evidenced by this page of minutes penciled by the secretary of the Sunday school of Echota Church, situated in the valley of Hummingbird Branch in western Adair County, Oklahoma. Oddly enough, after the memoranda are written, there is usually very little care exer-

---

[2] MS in collection of authors.
[1] His falling ill.
[2] MS in collection of authors.

cised in seeing that they do not become lost, defaced, or destroyed. The psychologist, no doubt, could interpret such inconsistency. We cannot.

August 9, 1959
ECHOTA SUNDAY SCHOOL

The Sunday School met.

In the beginning we sang; and also we used the children's prayer book;[1] and also the Chairman[2] read Philippians, Chapter 1, Verses 23 to 28; and then we prayed.

And then we began reading our Bibles. We read Second Timothy, Chapter 4, Verse 22; and then the Teacher read. Then he stopped reading, and he discussed it. Then he turned it over to anyone who had any questions about the first verse. It was questioned, and it was much discussed;[3] and the 16th Verse was also questioned, and it was understood.

Then the Treasurer called for[4] money—$.75 in all, and $2.73 for the Pastor's salary. The children collected $.20, *Birthday offering*.[5] It was voted to deduct $.56 for our indebtedness.[6]

SALO:LI BROODS OVER THE DESTINY OF THE CHEROKEES (1963)

The Oklahoma Cherokees have shared little in post-World War II prosperity. There is little industry in their territory; they possess a relatively small amount of land now; there is not much in their culture to attract the touristic camera with its attendant free-spending. They earn what cash they can by picking beans and berries for the white man and tending his

---

[1] This is obscure. We know of no such book in the Cherokee language. Perhaps the book was in English.

[2] The superintendent of the Sunday school.

[3] One may be sure of this.

[4] The literal Cherokee is not only more picturesque, but perhaps more accurate: a treasurer does not request money, he "hunts for" it.

[5] This custom, borrowed from the whites, is one whereby a member of the Sunday school who has had a birthday during the week preceding, on Sunday goes to the altar and deposits in a jar the number of pennies that corresponds to his age.

[6] MS in collection of authors.

cattle that roam over land that was once Cherokee allotments. They are among the very poorest people in the United States.

This jeremiad, written by someone named Salo:li in Mayes or Delaware County, is a somber picture of the present-day Cherokees limned by a Cherokee.

When the white-skinned man came across here to America, that is when the molestation of the Cherokee Indian began, and even up to this time the Cherokee Indian is still being made uneasy where he lives on this continent.

Now, starting in the year 1963, the Cherokee Indian is being made uneasy everywhere in the Cherokee country of Oklahoma. Now their land is being sold for them, and what is happening here in the Cherokee Nation is the same as that which happened when they lived in the East, in the Old Cherokee Nation at Chickamauga.[1] Then sometime later they were driven out. They were driven toward the West. Just as when John Ross brought the Cherokee Indian populace, the same thing is happening in Oklahoma.

Now for the Cherokee Indian there is nothing to turn to except the one thing left to do about these happenings—and that is to turn to God.[2]

LETTERS FROM A CHRISTIAN MEDICINE MAN (1963)

The writer of these two letters is perhaps the most esteemed of all contemporary Oklahoma Cherokee medicine men. A kindly, avuncular individual, his empirical knowledge of botany and plant chemistry is truly encyclopedic. But he has never driven an automobile, voted, nor seen a motion picture. He has seen television, but with considerable disappointment. His cabin in the woods, which he built himself, boasts neither electricity nor running water, and he neither wants nor misses them. His prize possession, monopolizing most of the space in one of his two small rooms, is an old upright piano which he cannot play.

[1] For some reason the settlements in the area of Chicamauga Creek in northern Georgia are thought of as the heart of the Old Cherokee Nation.
[2] MS in collection of authors.

If anyone—white, brown, or black—derives any pleasure or profit from twentieth-century living, Uwo:díge rejoices that he does; but as far as he is personally concerned, life principally consists of singing Christian hymns in Cherokee with any individual that he can entrap into carrying a part, and in healing men's hurts in ways that were perhaps already ancient when Moses raised his rod in the wilderness.

1.

August 26, 1963

Now! This evening I just wrote you, friend Tse:gi.

A very sad thing happened to us. This last Friday at Di:-ghalv:sadv:di[1] where he was working, on August 23rd, a big earth-shovel crushed and killed one of my in-laws.[2] They buried him last Sunday. We left[3] at that time.

It is truly sad that it happened to him. That is all that I wanted to tell you.

The survivors are all well, and I also am well, and I hope that you are well.

Now! That is all that I, Uwo:díge Gi:gage, just wrote. I greet you all: "Hello!"

2.

September 5, 1963

Now! Now I have sent you the medicine. Now this medicine he is first to rub upon himself. He is to smoke it later, for four days, and for four days he is to leave it alone, and then he is to start again (for four days)—and in doing it, that is the treatment.

All of us are getting along well. You must send me a letter.

I, Uwo:díge Gi:gage, just wrote this, Tse:gi, for you to read. I am sending my greetings to all: "Hello!"

They buried A:dátso:sd(a)'s brother today.

Now! That is all.[4]

---

[1] The Cherokee form of Strang, a town in Mayes County.
[2] His son-in-law.
[3] Left home and went to where the funeral was held.
[4] MSS in collection of authors.

Social Documents of the Cherokees, 1862–1964

A Baptist Minister's Dream (1963)

The ensuing was written in a manuscript book of conjurations by a Baptist preacher of Cherokee County, Oklahoma. The minister's late father was one of the most celebrated of conjurers; we doubt that at any time he ever professed belief in Christianity.

This same minister once told us that an intense yearning to see with his own eyes the glories of Solomon's Temple led to a dream of having done so. The view was less than prepossessing: the Temple was a log cabin.

November 1, 1963

On Friday night I dreamed that my late father, Tsa:li Di:hl(i)dhade:gi, and I talked with each other. I went to visit him where God lives.

He told me how long I will be living on earth. I still have some time left to be happy on top of the earth, and that is all the time I have in which to do kind works and to tell the Good Word to church organizations everywhere on earth. And if Jesus Christ thinks that I did the right thing, then at my father's place I will be living and rejoicing, and my father and I will be together.[1]

Gana:hw(i)so:sg(i) Recalls the World War I Parade Ground (1964)

The bewilderment and discomforts of the parade ground, reviewed in autumnal years, have a tendency to become encrusted with humor, whatever the race of the former serviceman. The Cherokee septuagenarian who amused himself by penciling these lines was one of the many hundreds of his tribe who when recruited for Mr. Woodrow Wilson's crusade possessed fully as much knowledge of the language (and perhaps the purposes) of their enemies as of their friends.

If many of the writer's tribesmen found death, glory, and a multitude of experiences lying between the two, on the battlefields of France, the writer did not. His shortcomings in the

---

[1] MS in collection of authors.

English language too much of an obstacle even for the rough-and-ready methods of top sergeants, his sole contribution to making the world safe for democracy was proffered in some camp in Georgia, a state that had not heard the sonorous Cherokee language since the writer's ancestors had been pillaged and sent into exile in 1838.

When I became a soldier, I did not know anything about soldier affairs. I could not speak the white man's language. I did not understand it, and I did not know the white man's books.[1]

I knew that when I was walking and making my turns, I was just stumbling around. When as we were going forward, we turned back, I kept on going. I bumped heads with the one who had turned—but the same thing happened to quite a few of us.

And when I put it[2] over my head, I did not do it right. You were supposed to put it in your mouth, and to put it over your nose. I put it tightly over my face. It cut off my breath. I took it off quickly.

When they gave us our guns, they asked me if I had cleaned mine. He[3] took it away from me and examined it. It was no good. When he returned it to me, he threw it to me. It hit me in the stomach. I was supposed to catch it.[4]

---

[1] He still can neither understand, speak, read, nor write English.
[2] Gas mask.
[3] The inspecting officer.
[4] MS in collection of authors.

Bibliography

Unpublished Material

Cherokee Nation Papers. University of Oklahoma Library. Norman, Okla.

Gadigwanasdi. "Original Formulae in Cherokee Syllabary from the Gadigwanasdi (Belt) Manuscript." MS No. 2590–a. Bureau of American Ethnology.

Inali [Inoli]. "Inali Formulae." MS No. 2236, Folder 1, Bureau of American Ethnology.

Inoli. "The Inoli Letters." MS No. 2241, Bureau of American Ethnology.

Kilpatrick, Anna Gritts, and Jack Frederick Kilpatrick. "Chronicles of Wolftown: Social Documents of the North Carolina Cherokees, 1850–1862." MS, scheduled for publication by the Bureau of American Ethnology in *Bulletin 196*.

Kilpatrick, Jack Frederick. "Echota Funeral Notices." MS, scheduled for publication by *Journal of the Graduate Research Center*, Southern Methodist University, Dallas, Texas.

Long, Will West. "Diary, Sept. 30, 1913–Aug. 17, 1914." MS, American Philosophical Library.

Mooney, James. "Letters in Cherokee Syllabary by Native Writers, 1887–92." MS No. 2241–b, Bureau of American Ethnology.

Russell, Mattie, "William Holland Thomas, White Chief of the Cherokees." doctoral dissertation, Duke University, 1951.

Swanton, John R. "The Panther and the Crane." MS No. 4227, Bureau of American Ethnology.

Wahnenauhi (Mrs. Lucy L. Keys). "Historical Sketches of the Cherokees: Together with Some of Their Customs, Traditions, and Superstitions." MS No. 2191, Bureau of American Ethnology. Scheduled for publication in *Bulletin 196*, Jack Frederick Kilpatrick, ed.

Published Material

Fogelson, Raymond D. "Change, Persistence, and Accommodation in Cherokee Medico-Magical Beliefs." In *Symposium on Cherokee and Iroquois Culture*, William N. Fenton and John Gulick, eds. Bureau of American Ethnology *Bulletin 180* (1961), 213–25.

———. Review of *Priests and Warriors: Social Structures of Cherokee Politics in the 18th Century*, by Fred Gearing. American Anthropological Association *Mem. 93* (Menasha, Wis., 1962). In *American Anthropologist*, Vol. 65, No. 2 (1963), 726–30.

Fogelson, Raymond D., and Paul Kutsche. "Cherokee Economic Cooperatives: The Gadugi." In *Symposium on Cherokee and Iroquois Culture*, William N. Fenton and John Gulick, eds. Bureau of American Ethnology *Bulletin 180* (1961), 83–121.

Foreman, Carolyn Thomas. *Park Hill*. Muskogee, Okla., 1948.

Gilbert, William Harlen, Jr. *The Eastern Cherokees*. Bureau of American Ethnology *Bulletin 133*, Anthropological Paper No. 23 (1943), 169–413.

Gulick, John. *Cherokees at the Crossroads*. Institute for Research in Social Science, University of North Carolina, Chapel Hill, 1960.

Hargrett, Lester. *Oklahoma Imprints, 1835–1890*. N.Y., 1951.

Kilpatrick, Jack Frederick. *The Siquanid Dil'tidegi Collection*. Bridwell Library, Southern Methodist University, Dallas, 1962.

———. "An Etymological Note on the Tribal Name of the Cherokees and Certain Place and Proper Names Derived from Cherokee." *Journal* of the Graduate Research Center, Southern Methodist University. Vol. 30, No. 1 (Dallas, 1962), 37–41.

———. "The Friends of Thunder," *Southwest Review*, Vol. 49, No. 2 (1963), 97–101.

Kilpatrick, Jack Frederick, and Anna Gritts Kilpatrick. "Plains Indian Motifs in Contemporary Cherokee Culture." *Plains Anthropologist*, Vol. 7, No. 16 (1962), 136–37.

———. " 'The Foundation of Life': The Cherokee National Ritual." *American Anthropologist*, Vol. 66, No. 6, Part I (1964), 1386–91.

———. *Friends of Thunder: Folktales of the Oklahoma Cherokees*. Dallas, 1964.

Bibliography

Mooney, James. "Sacred Formulas of the Cherokees." *7th Annual Report*, Bureau of American Ethnology (1891), 302–97.

———. *Myths of the Cherokee. 19th Annual Report*, Bureau of American Ethnology (1900), 3–576.

Mooney, James, and Frans M. Olbrechts. *The Swimmer Manuscript*. Bureau of American Ethnology *Bulletin 99* (1932).

Shirley, Glenn. *Law West of Fort Smith: Frontier Justice in the Indian Territory*. N.Y., 1961.

Starr, Emmet. *History of the Cherokee Indians and Their Legends and Folk Lore*. Oklahoma City, 1921.

Swanton, John R. *Myths and Tales of the Southeastern Indians*. Bureau of American Ethnology *Bulletin 88* (1929).

Thomas, Robert K. "The Redbird Smith Movement." In *Symposium on Cherokee and Iroquois Culture*, William N. Fenton and John Gulick, eds. Bureau of American Ethnology *Bulletin 180* (1961), 159–66.

Wardell, Morris L. *A Political History of the Cherokee Nation, 1838–1907*. Norman, 1938.

Williams, Samuel Cole. *Adair's History of the American Indians*. Johnson City, Tenn., 1930.

Woodward, Grace Steele. *The Cherokees*. Norman, 1963.

Index

Ada:ga, De:wi (delegate to Washington): 26
Adair, James: reports Cherokee treatment of smallpox, 15
Adair County, Okla.: 8n., 20, 44, 59, 61, 62, 76, 78, 81, 85, 103; MSS from, 46, 54, 89; conjuration from, 48
A:dátso:sd(a): brother of, dies, 106
Ada:wé:hi: 48n.
Ade:lagh(a)dhí:ya, E:gi: comes for baptism, 84
Ade:lagh(a)dhí:ya, Sa:li: appointed baker for convention, 85
AʔdhohiːsgI, Li:wi: appointed worker for convention, 86
Adho:lanv:sdi, Sdhi:wi: reports at quarterly meeting, 74
Ado:dhlvhi:soʔdhí:yi (ceremony): 88–89
Aghv:li, Tsi:sdv: approves Sunday school regulations, 67
Agiló:hi (survivor of soldier): 15
Agwade:gi (survivor of soldier): 15
Aha:ma[1]: chosen to obtain cow, 75
Aha:ma[2]: receives letter from Ghanvtsu:hwa Ne:di, 94

Ahu:yv (sister of I:no:li): I:no:li writes to, 17
AʔhwáⁱdayaːI: allotted land at Wolftown, 22
Aʔhw(i)gado:ga (Confederate soldier): issued clothing, 13
Aʔhw(i)gado:ga, De:wi: writes Uwe:da:sadh(i), 72–73
A:hyv́i:ní: notebook of, translated by Mooney and Olbrechts, 40; supplies myths to Mooney, 40; calligraphy of, 40–41; writes Mooney, 41
A:hyv́i:ní, Tsa:ts(i): nominated for sergeant-at-arms, 78
Akins (Sequoyah Co.), Okla.: 73n.
A:ligi: dies in epidemic at Qualla, 16
A:l(i)sa: writes Tso:saya, 37–39, 38n.
Ali:sini: reminded of debt, 39
A:matsv:na (Confederate soldier): issued clothing, 13
A:matsv:na, Sigwi:ya: owed by Le:gini, 20
Ama:y(i)gado:ga (Confederate soldier): listed as dead, 14
America: 105
American Philosophical Society, Library of: Cherokee medical writings in, 17

Index

A:mó:hi District: origin of name of, 71; *see also* Saline District

A:mó:hi Fire: collection of money by, 70–71

A:muno:yv:gi, Wo:yi: dying testimony of, 65

A:n(a)gwalu:v:sgi, Sa:dayi: comes for baptism, 84

An(a)sde:gwo (place name in Oklahoma): 55; *see also* Big Sticks

Ane:sgwade:gi (treasurer of A:mó:hi Fire): 71

Anidó:na? (Confederate soldier): listed as dead, 14

Ani:gidu:hwagi: 53n.; *see also* Keetoowah Society

Ani:tsa (survivor of soldier): 14; funeral notice of, 24–25

Aniyv:la, Ada:lo?di:sgi: changes church affiliation, 76

A:nuwe:gi (survivor of soldier): 15; allotted land at Wolftown, 22

Arkansas: 26n., 44; gospel songs published in, 74

Arkansas River: 93n.; ferry across, 72

Articles of Agreement (1730): 101

Asheville, N.C.: I:no:li writes from, 22–23, 23n.

Atsi:sgvhnagesdv́:yi ("Redhorse Domain-place"): 55n.; *see also* Illinois District

Auction sale: of effects of Dasgi:gidi:hi, 3–6; a custom in North Carolina and Oklahoma, 17; of effects of Ulo:-nagi:sgi, 18; a custom in Wolftown, 18

A:yele (survivor of soldier): 15

A:yi:yv:ha, Ge:di: 26

Ayo:hlani, Li:wi: 64n.

Ayo:hlani, Tsa:wayu:ga: dying testimony of, 63–64

Baptist church: 107; among Cherokees, 24; affection for, imputed to Mooney, 42; September convention of, 85; *see also* Cedar Tree Baptist Church, Echota Baptist Church, Fairfield Baptist Church, Honey Hill Baptist Church, Lees Creek Baptist Church, Mulberry Tree Baptist Church, New Baptist Church, Round Springs Baptist Church, Salem Baptist Church, Sequoyah Baptist Church, *and* Sycamore Tree Baptist Church

Barber (Cherokee Co.), Okla.: 72n., 84; *see also* Gwagwó:hi

Baron Fork of the Illinois River (Okla.): 54

Beamer, Louis: 34n.

Big Cove Township (N.C.): 32n., 42n.

Big Sticks: 55n.; *see also* An(a)sde:gwo

Bird, Peter: 63n.

Black (*Cassia marilandica*): 92 & n.

"Black, the": 48; conjuration for, 92n., 92–93

"Black yellow, the": 25

Buffington, Thomas M.: identification requested of, by Tsa:ni Do:yaní:si, 52n.,

113

52–53; *see also* Ganvhi:da, Da:mi
Bunch (Adair Co.), Okla.: 59; *see also* Tsegí:i
Bureau of American Ethnology: Cherokee MSS in, 3 & n., 17, 39n., 40; Natchez Cherokee myth in, 58
Bushyhead, Dennis Wolfe: 35n.; *see also* Tsunulv:hv:sgi

Cabin Creek, Battle of: 20
Canadian District: 34–35
Cardiac disease: prescription for, 82–83
Cedar Tree Baptist Church: 74
Cheowa: 36; residents of, visit troops, 8 & n.; recipient of letter probably resident of, 17; Tsa:ni Da:gwadi:hi writes from, 43
Cherokee, N.C.: 52
Cherokee County, Okla.: 61, 71, 72n., 84, 85, 88, 97, 103, 107; battle charm from, 46; medical prescription from, 83
Cherokee freedmen: contend for political rights, 34–35
Cherokee Hymn Book: 78, 82, 83
Cherokee Indians: honesty of, 4; style of letter writing of, 6n., 94; contentiousness of, 9; concern with *duyu:gh(o)dv* of, 9–10; duties of, as Confederate soldiers, 10–11; sense of humor of, 11; woodsmanship of, 11; smallpox among, 15; belief of, about their vulnerability to certain diseases, 16–17, 17n.; matricentered aspect of household of, 18; views of, on disposition of estates, 18–19; principle of ultimogeniture among, 19; mortuary customs of, 24; semeiology of, 25n.; revival meetings among, 32; aboriginal religion of, 36; self-image of, as peace-loving people, 45; battle charms of, 45–46; legal terminology of, 46; dichotomy in nature of, 50; Christians among, oppose nativistic movement, 53; family papers of, 54; accept fugitive Natchez, 57; chronology of, 59–60; payments to, 60n.; reverence of, for Ani:lage:yv Ugí:dahl(i), 62; dying testimony of Christians among, 63–65; mixed with Creeks at Eveningshade, 68; supreme ritual of, 68; clans of, 71n.; musical talent of, 74; singing practices of, 74–75; intramural politics of, 77; Christian hymns of, 78; medico-religious writings of, 80; "Going to the Water" rites of, 80–81; interest of, in botany, 82; medical prescriptions of, 82; temperance song of, 82; remedy for cardiac disease of, 82–83; condition of, in Great Depression, 84; divining practices of, 84n.; myths of, 96n.; emphasis upon import of dreams by, 97; surgery of, 98n.; views of, on eating fish, 100n.; chiefs of, visit England, 101; decoration of graves by, 102; "genius for institutionalization" of, 102; infant mor-

Index

tality among, 102; war dead of, 102; keeping of church and Sunday school records by, 103–104; molestation of, by white men, 105; in World War I, 107

Cherokee Nation: 20n., 29n., 32n., 44, 59, 60n., 76, 105n.; Civil War in, 3; slaveholding in, 4; white intruders in, 26, 28; corrupt officialdom in, 29; crop failures in, 33; interest in elections in, 34; 1881 National Council election in, 34–35; loss of records of district courts of, 44; Constitution of, 44; absence of citizens of, during enrollment, 52; Keetoowah "Fires" in, 56

Cherokee National Jail: 29n.

Cherokee Removal: 3, 8n., 82

Cherokee Temperance Society: organization of, 82

Cherry: Indian (*Rhamnus caroliniana*), in prescription for cardiac disease, 83 & n.; wild (*Prunus* sp.), in prescription for cardiac disease, 83 & n.

Chickamauga Creek (Ga.): 105n.

Christian religion: 24–25, 53, 61–67, 73–77, 78–80, 82, 83–85, 90, 102–104, 105–107

Civil War: participation of Cherokees in, 3; report of casualties in, 8; *see also* Government War

Claremore Indian Hospital: letters from patient in, 93–95

"Come, Humble Sinner" (Watts): Cherokee hymn not translation of, 83–84

Commissioner of Indian Affairs: 26

Company C, 69th N.C. Volunteer Infantry (the Thomas Legion): 16n.

Confederacy: 5n.; military morals of, objected to, 11; finances of, 13 & n.

Confederates: 3, 11n., 19n.

Conjuration: for muscular cramps, 48–50; book, of World War I soldier, 69; book, 91; for protruding navel, 91–92; for "the black," 92–93; book, from Cherokee County, 107

Conjurer: 71 & n., 107

Conjuring book: 32n.; *see also* conjurations

Conjuring ceremony: 71n., 89n.

Cooweescoowee (Guwi:sguwi) District: origin of name of, 32n.

Corn: importance of, to Cherokees, 34 & n.

Court (British): visited by Cherokees, 101

Creeks: receive fugitive Natchez, 57; mixed with Cherokees at Eveningshade, 68

Creek War: 26n., 60 & n.

Cumings, Sir Alexander: 101n.

Da:dhlvda (Confederate soldier): issued clothing, 14; *see also* Da:tsvda (dialectal variant)

Da:gi: 37

Dagv:wo?si: serves as member of Echota Sunday School committee, 77

Dagv:wo?si, Wali:ya: chosen as

cake baker by Echota Sunday
  School committee, 77
Da:gwadi:hi: supplies Mooney
  with conjurations and myths,
  42; receives letter from son at
  Cheowa, 43
Da:gwadi:hi, Ga:lanv:da: secretary of A:mó:hi Fire, 71
Da:gwadi:hi, Tsa:ni: writes to
  father, 42–43
Da:hw(i)sini (Confederate soldier): listed as dead, 15
Da:hw(i)sini, Tse:gi: 26
Da:sgigidi:hi (Confederate soldier): effects of, auctioned,
  4–5; listed as dead, 14
Da:tsvda: dies in epidemic at
  Qualla, 16; see also Da:dhlvda
  (dialectal variant)
Davis, Jefferson: 25
Dawes, Henry L. (chairman of
  Dawes Commission): 52
Dawes Commission: 52
Dawi:sgalv́:yi: see Flint District
De:gi: dies in epidemic at
  Qualla, 16
Delaware County, Okla.: 83,
  100, 105
Depression, Great: condition of
  Cherokees in, 84
De:wi, Gwe:di: dying testimony of, 64–65
Dhalu:gi:sgi, Tsvgh(a)dha:sdi:
  reminded of debt, 40
Dhla:nuwo:h(i): 66; see also
  Fairfield Baptist Church
Dhlvdi:sd(a) [1]: makes statement concerning runaway
  girl, 54–55
Dhlvdi:sd(a) [2]: acts as chairman of Echota Sunday School
  committee, 76

Dhlvdi:sd(i), Sina:sda: repents
  at quarterly meeting, 73
Dhotsu:hwa, Yo:nv́wi:n(v):
  writes to Sa:lada Tsa:ts(i), 91
Di:dagw(i): writes to Da:sgigidi:hi Digv:wa:sade:sgi,
  45
Dida:lidó:gi (Confederate soldier): issued clothing, 13
Di:gahl(u)ghwade:gi: allotted
  land at Wolftown, 22
Di:ghalv:sadv:di: 106; see also
  Strang (Mayes Co.), Okla.
Di:ghuyi:sgi (Confederate soldier): illness of, 5; allotted
  land at Wolftown, 22
Di:gini (Confederate soldier):
  issued clothing, 13
Digo:hw(a)dhi:sgi, Gwe:ni:
  contributes to Keetowah Society, 56
Digo:ye:sgi, Uwe:dhiyu:la: appointed worker for convention, 86
Digu:gh(o)di:sgi: chosen by
  Echota Sunday School to carry water, 76
Digv:ghe:hw(i)sdo:dhí:yi
  (type of incantation): 71n.
Digv:gi:sgi (Confederate soldier): listed as dead, 15
Digv:wa:sade:sgi, Da:gwadi:hi:
  receives letter from Di:dagw(i), 45
Di:hl(i)dhade:gi, Sighwani:da:
  appointed worker for convention, 86
Di:hl(i)dhade:gi, Tsa:li: record
  of dream about, 107
Di:lasge:sgi: reports commemoration of assassination of Lincoln, 25–26

Index

Di:ni:nv, Diga:sa:gwalv (judge of Goingsnake District): writes to Digu:hl(e)di:sgi Wa:dh(i), 47–48

Di:sdo:sgi, A:li: appointed baker for convention, 85

Divining: 63, 88–89, 89–90

Di:ye:lidó:hi (Confederate soldier): listed as dead, 14

Diwo:sgi (Confederate soldier): listed as dead, 15

Dla:ne:na, Dayi:ni (patient of medicine man): 89

Dloge:si, Sa:mi: preaches at Mulberry Tree Baptist Church, 76

Do:sagaya:sdi (Confederate soldier): listed as dead, 15

Do:tsulé:ʔhnv (Confederate soldier): counsels Tse:-gh(i)sini, 6; writes to I:no:li, 12

"Dove-place": *see* London, England

Dream: of medicine man, 97–98

Dreams: emphasis upon import of, 97

Duyu:gh(o)dv ("right"): 9n., 9–10; white man's version of, 19

Dvdi:sdv: allotted land at Wolftown, 22

Dv́:n(a)dé:dhon(i) (district judge): receives petition, 44–45

Dvni:gisi (Confederate soldier): listed as dead, 14

Dvno:hwe:la:ni, Tso:wa: transcribes regulations adopted by Sunday school of Fairfield Baptist Church, 67

Earthquake: 36, 60 & n.

Eastern Cherokees: 25, 52; in Civil War, 3; economic condition of, 4; in Graham County, N.C., 8n.; privations of, in Civil War, 12–13; war orphans among, issued clothing, 13; Confederate soldiers of, desert to Union, 15; government of, established, 22n., 36; in litigation with Will Thomas, 23; lend money, 39; receive livestock, 39n.; Su:ye:dv U:gu:ghu, chief of, 41; Poor-Aid Society of, 66; literacy among, 100

Echota Baptist Church: 44, 78; quarterly meeting at, 73–74; Sunday school of, makes plans, 75–76; receives letter from Mulberry Tree Baptist Church, 76; Sunday school of, decides upon cake sale, 76–77; host to convention, 85–86; pastor of, writes to one of his deacons, 103; minutes of Sunday school of, 103–104

Echota community (Adair Co., Okla.): belief of inhabitants of, concerning their descent, 44; notebook of household conjurations from, 91

Echota Methodist Mission (N.C.): 24, 32

E:gi: 26

E:lohi Ga:ghusdv:d(i) ("The Foundation of Life"): 68

England: 69

E:ni [1]: greeted by Tse:-gh(i)sini, 6, 9

E:ni [2] (survivor of soldier): 15

117

E:sigi: death of, 36
Eucha (Delaware Co.), Okla.: 73n.
Eveningshade (Sequoyah Co., Okla.): 68

Fairfield Baptist Church: 74; adopts Sunday school regulations, 66–67; *see also* Dhla:‐nuwo:h(i)
"Fires" (of Keetoowah Society): 55
Flint: use of, in surgery, 43n.
Flint District: 35, 63n.; origin of name of, 44; MSS from, 59
France: 69, 107
Funeral notices: 24–25, 67

Ga:dayó:sd(i): *see* Marble City (Sequoyah Co.), Okla.
Ga:dhidv: definition of, 98n.
Gadhi:yo: at home of Redbird Smith, 55; meaning of, 55n.; of Nv:ya Ghayv:sadv́:i Fire, 60; of A:mó:hi Fire, 71; moved to Marble City, 91
Ga:dhlinuli:sgi, Ganv:dho:hi: acts as one of chairmen of Memorial Day ceremony, 102
Gado:tsv:na (survivor of soldier): 14
Gado:yoe: receives letter from I:no:li, 23
Ga:du:gi: definition of, 75
Ga:gama (Confederate soldier): issued clothing, 13
Ga:gama, Digo:hisdi:sgi: death of, 50
Gahu:ni (Confederate soldier): issued clothing, 14
Galu:sadi:hi (Confederate soldier): issued clothing, 14

Gana:gilv, Ama:yigado:ga: reports illness of Ulo:nagi:sgi, 17
Gana:hw(i)so:sg(i): writes of experiences in World War I, 107–108
Gane:lv:sa: repents at quarterly meeting, 73
Ga?ni, Sa:mi: friendship of, with Di:dagw(i), 45
Ganvhi:da, Da:mi: 52; *see also* Buffington, Thomas M.
Ga:yani (Confederate soldier): listed as dead, 14
Ge:dini (Confederate soldier): in skirmish, 12
Ge:hyahi: petitions district judge, 44
Ge:layi:ni, E:sigi: estate of, disputed, 18–20
Georgia: 3, 60n., 105n.; Cherokee land in, surveyed, 60; military camp in, 108
Germany: 90
Ge:si: allotted land at Wolftown, 22
Gha:hl(i)se:ts(i) Tso:dalv Fire: collection of money by, 70
Gha?lada, E:gi: appointed baker for convention, 85
Gha:n(a)sgawi, Du:si: appointment of, as executor requested, 44
Ghane:ga: Ne:li: repents at quarterly meeting, 74
Ghani:ga: sorcery against requested, 71
Ghani:gwayo:gi, E:tsini: agrees to supply workers for convention, 85
Ghan(i)si:ni: death of, 18

Index

Ghanóhe:n(a) (Cherokee dish): preparation of, 60
Ghe:ladi (survivor of soldier): 14
Ghiyu:ga, Sali:ni: 37
Ghiyu:ga, Salo:li Utsv:da: I:no:li writes to, 36–37
Ghodé:sgi, Sali:gug(i): preaches at Memorial Day ceremony, 103
Gho:gv: debt to Le:gini, 20; reminded of debt, 39
Gho:lanv́:yi: 32n.; *see also* Raven-place
Gh(u)wayó:hi: 100 & n.; *see also* Pryor (Mayes Co.), Okla.
Ghu:wv, I:nagi: preaches at Memorial Day ceremony, 103
Ghv:he [1] (survivor of soldier): 14
Ghv:he [2] (survivor of soldier): 15
Ghv:hwisi:da (Cherokee dish): 96
Ghv?sa?ni: repents at quarterly meeting, 74
Gi:gage, Uwo:díge: sketch of, 105–106; writes Tse:gi[2], 106
Godagwa:sgi (Confederate soldier): listed as dead, 15
Going Snake (Cherokee leader): 26n.
Goingsnake District: 20, 29, 44, 55; solicitor of, resigns, 26n., 26–28; citizens of, petition Utsale:dv, 33–34; judge of, writes Digu:hl(e)di:sgi Wa:dh(i), 47–48
"Going to the Water": 46n., 80–81, 89

Go:liwa:ni: dies in epidemic at Qualla, 16
Gore (Sequoyah Co.), Okla.: 72
Government War: 60 & n.; *see also* Civil War
Graham County, N.C.: affinity of Cherokees in, 8n.
Grand River (Okla.): salines along, 71
Gu:le-disgo:hnihi: *see* London, England
Gv:hnidv (Confederate soldier): listed as dead, 14
Gv:na (Confederate soldier): listed as dead, 14
Gvwahyu:da (survivor of soldier): 14
Gwagwó:hi: 72n.; *see also* Barber (Cherokee Co.), Okla.
Gwe:dh(i)si: dies in epidemic at Qualla, 16
Gwe:di: allotted land at Wolftown, 22
Gwe:gi: hoe bought from, by E:sigi Ge:layi:ni, 19
Gwe:ni (Confederate soldier): issued clothing, 13

Haley's Comet: 60n.
Ha:li (Confederate soldier): listed as dead, 14
He:nil(i), Tsu:wi: 94
He:nilv, A:dawi: receives letter from Dhotsu:wha Sighwani:-da, 68; receives letter from Lu:si O:gan(a)sdo:da, 93 & n.
Hi:yiné:i, Adi:dhlidó:hi: petitions district judge, 44
Hi:yiné:i, Ne:ni: petitions district judge, 44
Honey Hill Baptist Church: 65
"Huckleberry-place": *see*

119

Gh(u)wayó:hi *and* Pryor (Mayes Co.), Okla.
Hummingbird Branch (Adair Co., Okla.): 44
Hungry Mountain (Cherokee Co., Okla.): 83
Hv:gi (survivor of soldier): 15
Hv:wo:di: dies in epidemic at Qualla, 16
Hv:wo:ni:sgi: dies in epidemic at Qualla, 16
Hv:yvli (survivor of soldier): 14

Illinois District: 55, 68, 91 & n.; *see also* Atsi:sgvhnagesdv́:yi
Illinois Fire: receives funds collected by other Fires, 70–71
Illinois River (Okla.): 55n.
Ilo:gwi (French place name?): 69 & n.
I:nadanaí:yi: 26n.; *see also* Goingsnake District
I:nadv (Confederate soldier): listed as dead, 15
Indian Home Guards: purchases by widow of fallen soldier in, 20–21
Indians: enrollment of, and allottment to, 52; colony of, near Tenkiller Lake, 57
Indian Territory: 52
I:no:li: 5n., 11n., 17n., 38n., Tse:gh(i)sini writes to, 3–6, 6–9; Tso:na writes to, 9–10; Do:tsulé:ʔhnv writes to, 10–12; issues clothing to soldiers and war orphans, 12–15; joins Thomas Legion, 13n.; records deaths from epidemic at Qualla, 15–16, 16n.; disposes of affairs of Ulo:nagi:sgi, 16–18; reports death of Ghan-(i)si:ni, 18; records dispute over estate, 18–20; records appointment of land at Wolftown, 21–22; allotted land at Wolftown, 22; writes from Asheville, 22–23, 23n.; looks up death records, 36–37; requested to read letter to Tso:saya, 39 & n.
"Inoli Letters, The": 7
Isa:yi, Tso:sgayoyoyí:yi: 89
I:sda: 98
I:sili: accepts Christianity, 84
Itsodí:yi (Cherokee dialect): 8n.

Jackson, Andrew: 60n.
Jackson County, N.C.: 7; I:no:li writes for Cherokees living in, 17; debts in, owed by Le:gini, 20
Jesus Christ: 59, 62
Jones, Evan: 53
Jones, John Buttrick: 53
Junaluska: 35n.

Keetoowah Society: 68; origin of, 53; address upon, 53; Se:dí:hi Fire contributes to, 55–57; dish prepared at meetings of, 60–61; official of Nv:ya Ghayv:sadv́:i Fire of, writes to official of Se:dí:hi Fire of, 60–61; A:mó:hi Fire of, 70; Gha:hl(i)se:ts(i) Tso:dalv Fire of, 70; letter from chief of, 90–91, 91n.; letter to official of, 93
Knoxville, Tenn.: 6n.
Korean War: Cherokee dead in, 102

Index

La:hw(i)sini (Confederate soldier): illness of, 6; visited in camp, 8; dies in epidemic at Qualla, 16
Latin Americans: 102
Lees Creek Baptist Church: 73
Le:gini: disputes with son over estate, 18–20
Li:di (survivor of soldier): 15
Li:la (survivor of soldier): 15
Lincoln, Abraham: 8n.; report of commemoration of assassination of, 25n., 25–26
London, England: 101n.
"Long-place": 56n.; *see also* Long Prairie
Long Prairie: 55, 56n.; *see also* "Long-place"
Lords Commissioners: make alliance with Cherokees, 101
"Lord's Door, The": sung in revival, 83–84
Love incantations: 70

McCarthy, W. C. (agent for Eastern Cherokees): 39n.
Marble City (Sequoyah Co.), Okla.: 91 & n.; *see also* Ga:-dayó:sd(i)
Mayes County, Okla.: 105, 106n.
Medical prescription (for cardiac disease): 82–83
Medical ritual (from Se:lamí:yi): 48–50
Medicine man: 5n., 12n., 32n., 40–41, 42n., 42–43, 48 & n., 68–69; secretiveness of, 43; diagnosis of, 88–89; dream of, 97–98
Me:li: 99
Memorial Day: regulations for observance of, 102–103

Methodist church: I:no:li minister of, 5n.; among Cherokees, 24; Wolftown revival notice of, 32–33, death of minister of, 36
Meuse-Argonne, Battle of: 69
Mink, Candy: spring named for, 50
Missouri Pacific Railroad: 72
Mooney, James: 41n.; on Cherokee casualties, 13; on origin of smallpox epidemic at Qualla, 15; affection of Cherokees for, 40; letters to, by A:hyvi:ní and Su:ye:dv U:gu:ghu, 40–42; supplied conjurations and myths by Da:gwadi:hi, 42n., 42–43; on "Going to the Water" ceremonies, 80–81
Mortuary customs: 24, 66, 66n., 102–103
Moytoy: 101n.
Mulberry Hollow (Adair Co., Okla.): 76
Mulberry Tree Baptist Church: sends letter to Echota Baptist Church, 76
Muskogee County, Okla.: 72n., 93n.
Myths: 57–59, 59n., 95–96

Natchez Cherokees: *see* Natchez Indians
Natchez Indians: war of, with French, 57; colony of, among Cherokees, 57; language of, 57; Swanton collects myths from, 57–58
Ne:di [1] (Confederate soldier): issued clothing, 13

Ne:di [2] (survivor of soldier): 14
Ne:di, Ghanvtsu:hwa: writes Sida:ni Ne:di, 93–95
Nedi, Sida:ni: receives letters from Ghanvtsu:hwa Ne:di, 93–95
Ne:ni [1] (survivor of soldier): 14
Ne:ni [2]: petitions district judge, 44
Ne:n(i)si (Ne:n(i)si Gana:gilv?): dies in epidemic at Qualla, 16
Nequassee: 101n.
Ne?sini: serves as member of Echota Sunday School committee, 77
Ne:tsili (survivor of soldier): 14
Ne:wadv, Gane:nu:li:sgi: resigns as solicitor, 26–28
New Baptist Church: 74
New Echota (Cherokee Nation, East): 44; *Cherokee Hymn Book* printed at, 78; Cherokee Temperance Society organized at, 82
New Jersey tea (*Ceanothus herbaceus*): in prescription for cardiac disease, 83 & n.
New Testament: translation of "save" in, 54n.
Ni:gi (Confederate soldier): listed as dead, 14
Ni:gudayi (survivor of soldier): 14
Nigula:ni: dies in epidemic at Qualla, 16
Nofire Hollow (Adair Co., Okla.): collection of papers from, 59
North Carolina: 3; Thomas Legionnaires arrive in, 11; law prohibiting Cherokee ownership of land in, 21; Cherokee delegation from, 26
North Carolina Cherokees: 18n.; use of wood-ash lye by, 17; land of, in litigation, 21
Nuwo:dhvn(a), Do:yi: nominated for sergeant-at-arms, 78
Nuwo:dhvn(a), La:wan(i): preaches at Memorial Day ceremony, 103
Nv:do: 41n.; *see also* Mooney, James
Nv:gi: reminded of debt, 39
Nv:tsi: requested to pray by A:li Usana:li, 63
Nv:ya Ghayv:sadv́:i (Adair Co., Okla.): meeting place of Keetowah Society, 55–57; *see also* "Stone Nose-place" *and* Stony Point

Oga?hnawa (Confederate soldier): listed as dead, 15
O:gan(a)sdo:da, Lu:si: writes to A:dawi [He:nilv], 93
O:hla, De:nili: heirs of, petition district judge, 44–45
O:hla, Tsa:ni: 95
Oklahoma: 26n., 99; Cherokee churches in, 24; Cherokee mortuary customs in, 24; eastern, infrequency of seismic phenomena in, 36; steps in preparation for statehood of, 52; the Cherokee Sunday school in, 66; transportation difficulties in Cherokee country of, 72; "Going to the Water" prayer from, 80–81
Oklahoma Cherokees: Sunday

Index

school organizations of, 66; hew ties for livelihood, 70; theft of timber from allotments of, 96–97; Christianity today among, 103; poverty of, 104–105

Olbrechts, Frans M.: finishes Mooney's work on notebook of A:hyv́i:ní, 40; on "Going to the Water" ceremonies, 80–81

Old-age assistance: concern of diarist about, 99

Owl, George: 41n.

O:yasdv: allotted land at Wolftown, 22

Painttown, N.C.: revival meetings at, 32

Parker, Judge Isaac C.: 29n.

Pennsylvania Avenue (Washington, D.C.): 41

"Pigeon-place": *see* London, England

Porum (Muskogee Co.), Okla.: 72 & n.

Proctor, Ezekiel ("Zeke"): 29, 32n.; *see also* Tsv:sgayo:o Sali:gug(i)

Pryor (Mayes Co.), Okla.: 100n.

Qualla, N.C.: 5n., 6n., 7, 7n., 8n., 22, 37; duties of troops from, 11; privations of homefolk at, 13; epidemic at, 15–16; Ulo:nigi:sgi, ill, comes to, 17; bartering economy at, 20; apportionment of land at, 21–22; churches at, 24; visited by Mooney, 40; wage scale at, 41; Mooney resides with Su:-ye:dv U:gu:ghv at, 41

Rabbit (place name in North Carolina): 5 & n.

Railroad ties: hewing of, Cherokee industry, 70

Raven-place: revival meetings at, 32 & n.; *see also* Gho:lanv́:-yi

Revival meetings: 32

Robbinsville, N.C.: 43

Root, medicinal: sent to I:no:li by Do:tsulé:ʔhnv, 12 & n.

Rose, wild (*Rosa carolina*): in prescription for cardiac disease, 83 & n.

Ross, John: 3, 32n., 60n., 105

Round Springs Baptist Church: 73

Sa:dayi (survivor of soldier): 15; owed by Le:gini, 20

Sagho:nige: informs Tsv:sgayo:o Sali:gug(i) of grand jury action, 29

St. Charles Hotel (Washington, D.C.): 41

St. Louis and San Francisco Railroad: 72

St. Mihiel, Battle of: 69

Salem Baptist Church: 62, 64n., 65

Sa:li: 23

Sali:gug(i), Tsv:sgayo:o: writes to Utsale:dv, 28–32; *see also* Proctor, Ezekiel ("Zeke")

Sali:gu:wa, Go:dhane: appointed baker for convention, 85

Sali:gu:wa, Unv:dagwv: ap-

pointed baker for convention, 86
Saline District: origin of name of, 71; *see also* A:mó:hi District
Saliva: symbolic washing with, 46 & n.
Sallisaw (Sequoyah Co.), Okla.: 74n.
Salo:lani: allotted land at Wolftown, 22
Salo:li: comments upon state of the Cherokees, 104–105
Salo:lu:gam(a) (Cherokee dish): preparation of, 60–61
Sa:wali, Uwe:da:sadh(i): receives letter from De:wi A?hw(i)gado:ga, 72–73; writes to unknown recipient, 96–97
Scratching, medical: in treatment for muscular cramps, 50 & n.
Sdhu:gado:ga (Confederate soldier): witnesses payment by Tse:gh(i)sini, 5 & n.; *see also* Sdhugi:gado:ga
Sdhugi:gado:ga: listed as dead, 14; *see also* Sdhu:gado:ga
Sdui:sdi, Uhyv:dhlo:yi: acts as one of chairmen of Memorial Day ceremony, 102
Se:dí:hi: 55 & n.
Se:dí:hi Fire: collects money for food, 55–57; official of, receives note from official of Nv:ya Ghayv:sadv́:i Fire, 60–61
Se:lamí:yi: 48
Seli:si: accepts Christianity, 85
Se:luwo:ya (Confederate soldier): issued clothing, 13

Sequoyah: 60 & n.
Sequoyah Baptist Church: 74
Sequoyah County, Okla.: 72n., 91n.; MS from, 68
Sequoyah syllabary: 4, 24, 25, 41n., 42, 48, 62, 69, 93, 96; Natchez Cherokee myth transcribed into, 58; hymns in, 75; literacy in, 100
Sgali:lo:sgi (Confederate soldier): listed as dead, 15
Sgaye:tsa, Diga?lisgi: appointed worker for convention, 86
Shaman: 12n., 40, 61, 69, 88, 97, 100; *see also* medicine man
Sida:ni: 65 & n.
Si?duwe:gi (Confederate soldier): listed as dead, 14
Siga:wi: preaches in revival at Sycamore Tree Church, 84
Sighwani:da, Dhotsu:hwa: 53, 68; *see also* Smith, Redbird
Si:gwitsi, Salo:li: receives letter, 100
Sina:sdhv (survivor of soldier): 14
Smallpox: epidemics of, among Cherokees, 15–16
Smith, Rev. Leslie: 24n.
Smith, Nimrod Jarrett: 41n.; *see also* Tsa:ladi:hi
Smith, Redbird: leader of "Nighthawk" movement, 53, 55, 61; writes A:dawi He:nilv, 68; *see also* Sighwani:da, Dhotsu:hwa
Smithsonian Institution: 40
Smoky Mountains: 3, 7n., 11
Snowbird Creek (N.C.): 8n.
Soco Creek (N.C.): 24
Solicitor, district: 26n.; *see also* Proctor, Ezekiel ("Zeke")

Index

Solomon's Temple: 107
South Carolina: no Cherokee settlements in (1867), 17
Stilwell (Adair Co.), Okla.: 66, 73n., 74n., 76, 99
"Stone Nose-place": 55n.; *see also* Nv:ya Ghayv:sadv́:i *and* Stony Point
Stony Point: 55; *see also* Nv:ya Ghayv:sadv́:i *and* "Stone Nose-place"
Strang (Mayes Co.), Okla.: 106n.; *see also* Di:ghalv:sadv:di
Strawberry Plains, Tenn.: 4, 7, 10n.
Sugar Mountain: 72, 97
Suge:da, Li:si: appointed baker for convention, 85
Su:le (Confederate soldier): death of, 6
Su:li, A:dawi: repents at quarterly meeting, 73
Susa:ni [1]: nominates Tsa:ts(i) A:hyv́i:ní for sergeant-at-arms, 78
Susa:ni [2]: 94, 95
Sv:ghi, Ghe:n(i)di: necrology by, 50–52; *see also* Mink, Candy
Sv:ghi, Tso:ni: death of, 50–52
Sv:na, Nuwo:hiyu: repents at quarterly meeting, 74
Swaney, N.C.: 42
Swanton, John R.: collects Natchez Cherokee myths, 57–58; phonetic system of, 58
Sycamore Tree Baptist Church: election of sergeants-at-arms at, 77–78; revival at, 83–85; agrees to supply workers for convention, 85–86

Sycamore Tree Cemetery: regulations for observance of Memorial Day at, 102–103

Tahlequah (Cherokee Co.), Okla.: 26n., 29n., 74n., 87, 99, 103
Tahlequah District: 29 & n., 34; probable epidemic in, 45; geographical relationship of, to Saline District, 71
Tenkiller Lake: 72n., 84; colony of Indians near, 87
Tennessee: 3; Thomas Legionnaires leave, 11; gospel songs published in, 74
Texas: 69; gospel songs published in, 74
"Thinkers": 89
Thomas, William Holland ("Will"): colonel of Thomas Legion, 3 & n.; informs troops of movement, 7n., 7–8; purchases clothing for Cherokees, 13 & n.; Qualla holdings of, in litigation, 21; sued by members of Eastern Band, 23
Thomas Legion: 11n.; North Carolina Cherokees in, 3; members of, blunder, 10–12; Company C of, 13 & n.; Su:ye:dv U:gu:ghv lieutenant in, 41
Thompson, Charles: 26 & n., 28, 32n.; petitioned by citizens of Goingsnake District, 33–34, 34n.
358th Infantry Regiment: 83
Thunder: 27 & n.
Timi: 26
Treaty of New Echota: 3

Tsadha:g(a)nihyv:ga: dies in epidemic at Qualla, 16

Tsa:ladi:hi: requested by A:hyvi:ní to read letter to Mooney, 41; as intermediary, receives letter from Su:ye:dv U:gu:ghu, 41

Tsa:li [1] (Confederate soldier): listed as dead, 14

Tsa:li [2]: allotted land at Wolftown, 22

Tsa:ni: 64

Tsa:n(i)la:tsi (Confederate soldier): issued clothing, 13; allotted land at Wolftown, 22

Tsan(i)lo:si (Confederate soldier): illness of, 6

Tsa:n(i)sini, Tsv:go:na: repents at quarterly meeting, 73

Tsa:ts(a) (Confederate soldier): listed as dead, 15

Tsa:ts(i): makes request of I:no:li, 37

Tsa:ts(i), Sa:lada: receives letter from Yo:nvwi:n(v) Dhotsu:hwa, 90–91

Tse:gh(i)sini [1]: 16n.; conducts auction of effects of Da:sgigidi:hi, 3–6; writes I:no:li on various matters, 6–9

Tse:gh(i)sini [2]: nominates Ditsuda:sgi Wi:li for sergeant-at-arms, 78

Tse:gi [1]: 26

Tse:gi [2]: receives letters from Uwo:díge Gi:gage, 106

Tsegi:i: 81; *see also* Bunch (Adair Co.), Okla.

Tse:gwadi:hi (Confederate soldier): issued clothing, 13; death of, 37

Tsiga:dhuhwi:sdi: 95

Tsígo:ne:la: vision of, and death of, 59

Tsi:guwi (survivor of soldier): 14

Tsimi: debt of, to Le:gini, 20

Tsi:mi, Tsa:yi: appointed worker for convention, 86

Tsi:ni: allotted land at Wolftown, 22

Tsi:sdu: 99

Tsi:sghwa, De:nili: dying testimony of, 63

Tsi:sghwa, Si:midhi: repents at quarterly meeting, 74

Ts(i)sgili (Confederate soldier): issued clothing, 13; chief of Wolftown, allotted land, 22

Ts(i)sgo:yi: dies in epidemic at Qualla, 16

Tsiyv:lv:da (survivor of soldier): 14

Tso?idi:h(i), Tsa:wayu:ga: witnesses contract, 47

Tso?idi:h(i), U:daniyv:dv: witnesses contract, 47

Tso:na (Confederate soldier): writes I:no:li, 9–10; dies in epidemic at Qualla, 16

Tso:saya: 37n., 38n.; directed by I:no:li to plant wheat, 23 & n.; receives letter from wife, 37–39

Tso:wa [1] (Confederate soldier): recovers from illness, 6

Tso:wa [2]: serves as secretary of Sycamore Tree Baptist Church and Sunday school, 86

Tso:wa [3]: 95

Tso:wa, Tsiyo:se: appointed baker for convention, 85

Index

Tsuda:sodi (Confederate soldier): listed as dead, 14

Tsu:di: misappropriates Tso:na's salt, 10 & n.

Tsughilv:di: accepts Christianity, 84

Tsugv:wahl(o)di: definition of, 38n.

Tsu:hla (Confederate soldier): issued clothing, 13; death of mother of, 37

Tsulio:wa: reindicted by grand jury, 29

Tsulo:gila (survivor of soldier): 14; dies in epidemic at Qualla, 16

Tsumi (Confederate soldier): witnesses payment by Tse:gh(i)sini, 5 & n.; listed as dead, 15

Tsu:n(a)ghilv́:di: 95

Tsu:n(a)sdu:di: serves as acting secretary of Echota Sunday School committee, 77

Tsu:n(a)sdu:di, Adawo:sgi: appointed worker for convention, 86

Tsu:n(a)sdu:di, Gadu:yui: appointed baker for convention, 85

Tsu:n(a)sdu:di, Ghe:ladi: chosen as cake baker by Echota Sunday School committee, 77

Tsu:n(a)sdu:di, La:yili: appointed baker for convention, 85

Tsu:n(a)sdu:di, Tsinv:na: appointed baker for convention, 85

Tsu:n(a)sdu:di, Tso:wa: appointed worker for convention, 86

Tsuna:walo:di: contributes to Keetoowah Society, 56

Tsunulv:hv:sgi: 35 & n.; *see also* Bushyhead, Dennis Wolfe

Tsu:sghwali:sd(a), Tsi:mi: dream concerning, 98

Tsu:tsayo: sdi, Su:ye:dv: appointed worker for convention, 86

Tsutso:ladha (Confederate soldier): issued clothing, 14; allotted land at Wolftown, 22

U:dan(i)dhu:da (Confederate soldier): listed as dead, 14

U:dhlvna:da (Confederate soldier): issued clothing, 14

Udi:sadiye:dv, Daye:ni: nominates Do:yi Nuwo:dhvn(a) for sergeant-at-arms, 78

Udi:sga?hli, Ne:si: repents at quartcrly meeting, 74

U:do:lanv:sdi, Sawa:ni: witnesses contract, 47

Ú:galo:gá: 59

U:gama (Confederate soldier): witnesses payment by Tse:gh(i)sini, 5

Ugí:dahl(i), Ani:lage:yv: 64n.; manuscripts written by, 62–63; sketch of life and work of, 62–63; summary of year's work by, 65n., 65–66

U:gi:sdi: definition of, 49n.

U:gu:ghu, Su:ye:dv: Mooney resides with, 41 & n.; writes Mooney, 42

U:hno:gv: 29

U:hwadhi: 65

Uhyalu:ga: mother of, witnesses for Tsa:ni Do:yaní:si, 52

Ule:na:hi (Confederate soldier): listed as dead, 15

Ule:so:dv: 32

Ule:yoe: dies in epidemic at Qualla, 16

Uli:da:sdi (Confederate soldier): listed as dead, 14

U:l(i)sdu:hi (Confederate soldier): issued clothing, 13; alloted land at Wolftown, 22

U:l(i)se?go:gí:dv: allotted land at Wolftown, 22

Ul(i)sga:sdi (survivor of soldier): 15

Ulo:nigi:sgi: 17n.; death and burial of, 16–18

Unedo:lv, Gho:ga: receives letter from Tso:wa Gan(i)si:ni U:ne:sdala, 34–35

Une:gada, Suda:ni: acts as one of chairmen of Memorial Day ceremony, 102

U:ne:sdala: chosen by Echota Sunday School to fry meat, 76; sketch of, 78–79; hymn book of, 79–80; temperance song by, 82

U:ne:sdala, Tso:wa Gan(i)si:ni: writes Gho:ga Unedo:lv, 34–35

Uni:nidu:yv, Ge:hida: 37

Union: 8n.; sympathizers with, hunted by Thomas Legion, 10; officers of, object to use of Cherokee soldiers, 11; *see also* United States

Unionists: 11n.

United States: role of, in North Carolina Cherokee land litigation, 21; Marshal, 29; Court, Western District of Arkansas, 29n.; Dawes Commission created by, 52; on brink of war, 68

Usana:li, A:li: dying testimony of, 63

U:sgogi:d(a): Lu:si O:gan(a)sdo:da reports on condition of, 93 & n.

U:sguni: authorized to receive money from Mooney, 41

Utsale:dv: receives letter of resignation from Gane:nu:li:sgi Ne:wadv, 26–28; receives letter from Ezekiel ("Zeke") Proctor, 28–32; receives petition from citizens of Goingsnake District, 33–34

Utse:nadha: allotted land at Wolftown, 22

Utsi:tsadh(a), E:lini: defaults on debt to Digu:hl(e)di:sgi Wa:dh(i), 47

Utsi:tsadh(a), Ne:n(i)si: seeks advice from judge of Goingsnake District, 47–48

Utso:sdo:sa: reports at quarterly meeting, 73

U:wawo:sida: allotted land at Wolftown, 22

V:ghini:li: definition of, 8n.

Wa:dh(i), A:li: list of purchases by, 20–21, 21n.

Wa:dh(i), Digu:hl(e)di:sgi: lends money to E:lini Utsi:tsadh(a), 47; receives letter from judge of Goingsnake District, 47–48; receives letter from Daye:wa Wahhya, 61

Index

Wa:di: chosen by Echota Sunday School to obtain cow, 75
Wadi:sgi, A:li (survivor of soldier): 15
Wahhya, Da:gi: 101
Wahhya, Daye:wa: writes to Digu:hl(e)di:sgi Wa:dh(i), 61
Wahhya, Tsa:ni: rents land from Me:li, 99
Wahhyaní:da (Confederate soldier): listed as dead, 15
Wa:lel(a), Tsi:mi: acts as chairman of Echota Sunday School committee, 77
Wali:sa (survivor of soldier): 14
Wa:li:si: requests sorcery directed against Ghani:ga, 71
"Walnut-place": *see* Se:dí:hi
Washington, D.C.: Mooney in, receives letter from Su:ye:dv U:gu:ghu, 41
Wa:sida?ni (Confederate soldier): issued clothing, 14; allotted land at Wolftown, 22
Watie-Boudinot faction: 3
Watts, Isaac: 83
Webbers Falls (Muskogee Co.), Okla.: 93 & n.
We:liní:i: 72n.; *see also* Welling (Cherokee Co.), Okla.
Welling (Cherokee Co.), Okla.: 72 & n.

Western Cherokees: in Civil War, 3; economic condition of, 4, 20; smallpox epidemics among, 15; literacy among, 15
Wi:li, Ditsuda:sgi: nominated for sergeant-at-arms, 78
Wi:ligi (Confederate soldier): recovery from illness of, 6
Wi:l(i)sini: allotted land at Wolftown, 22; 23
Wilson, Woodrow: 107
Wolf Clan: 71
Wolftown, N.C.: 7 & n., 17n., 32n.; list of residents of, who died, 15–16; auction sales in, 18; land apportioned in, 21–22; Methodists in, 32; I:no:li guard and clerk of, 36; vital statistics kept at, 36; town council of, sets interest rates, 39
World War I: Cherokees in, 68–69, 83, 107–108
World War II: 70, 94n., 104; comment upon, 90
Wo:yigvgi:sdi (Confederate soldier): issued clothing, 14

Yankees: killed by Thomas Legionnaires, 11 & n.
"Yellow, the": 48, 92n.
Yo:nv, Uwe:da:sadh(i): 32

The text for *The Shadow of Sequoyah* has been set in Linotype Janson, a charming book face bearing the name of its founder, Anton Janson of Leipzig. Two sizes of type are utilized in the text, ten-point for the commentaries, and eleven-point for the letters. Two points of space between lines give added legibility. The paper on which the book is printed bears the watermark of the University of Oklahoma Press and has an effective life of at least three hundred years.

Augsburg College
George Sverdrup Library
Minneapolis, Minnesota 55404